IT TAKES GUTS

A MEAT-EATER'S
GUIDE TO EATING OFFAL

WITH OVER **75** **HEALTHY & DELICIOUS**

NOSE-TO-TAIL RECIPES

VICTORY BELT PUBLISHING INC.

LAS VEGAS

Cover design by Charisse Reyes

Cover photography by Amy Zambonin

Interior design by Charisse Reyes and Crizalie Olimpo

Food photography by Heather MacDonald

Illustrations on pages 5, 6, 8, 12, 24, 29, 35, 38, 41, 48, 51, 73, 95, 97, 119, 143, 165, 181, 205, 232, 236, and 253 by Patty Toner

Additional illustrations by Allan Santos

Printed in Canada

TC 0120

TABLE OF CONTENTS

FOREWORD

I will never forget meeting Ashleigh VanHouten. I have spent over a decade in the fitness and wellness space, and to this day it is dominated by male figures in leadership positions. It was nice to meet a woman who brought the same strength and charisma, and who can hold her own simply being who she is.

We met at an event in which she was interviewing other experts in the wellness field. Ashleigh was part of a team of two other guys, and within fifteen minutes, it felt like we were old friends, and indeed we would become that.

There is a lot I admire about "The Muscle Maven." Frankly, she is one of a kind with an extremely adventurous spirit, which can easily be seen in the pages of this book. Ashleigh does an incredible job at taking foods often thought of as taboo and intimidating (at least in some parts of modern Western culture) and making them palatable and enjoyable for the mainstream, while also helping us understand the nutritional aspects to these choices.

The value of this cookbook does not stop at the novelty of eating things that are outside of our comfort zone. What is provided here is a road map to the most nutrient-dense and prized food of our ancestors. In the following pages, you will find some of the world's original superfoods.

Protein in all animal-based forms is the most essential macronutrient—and yet deeply controversial, because this food source has a face. As such, it is often the most overlooked macronutrient, and often the proverbial black sheep. **Well, it is time to eat the sheep—all of it.**

In today's world, we are up against the clock, domestication, and inactivity combined with diseases of aging that run the gamut of insulin resistance, obesity, hypertension, cardiovascular disease, and even dementia. During my seven years of training in nutritional science (which included a two-year combined research/clinical fellowship at Washington University in geriatrics/ obesity medicine and nutritional science), as well as my previous medical training and continued mentorship with one of the world-leading protein experts, the concept of Muscle-Centric Medicine was born. This is the concept that we are not over-fat, but rather under-muscled. I bring this up because on a fundamental level, dietary protein is the solution to these diseases of aging, yet we are up against a narrative of eating more plants and reducing animal protein as both the healthier and more "moral" choice. This is the single worst piece of advice I've seen as a clinician; the solution is to find more creative and sustainable ways to include all parts of the animal, and Ashleigh has done that here.

Protein is necessary for healthy, youthful muscle. Muscle is important in metabolic regulation; in fact, it determines a large part of your resting metabolic rate and is your metabolic currency. By optimizing muscle tissue through dietary protein, one can optimize the organ of longevity, which is muscle.

For the longest time, when I thought of protein, I only thought of the "meat." I will never forget when Ashleigh took me to a restaurant in New York City where they served a true nose-to-tail selection. Naturally, my husband, who is a ten-year Navy SEAL with multiple deployments under his belt, turned to me and said, "Honey, other cultures eat way more than the meat." So of course, I ordered from the menu what seemed to be the safest: sweetbreads. It turns out that sweetbreads are actually pancreas and thymus, and while I initially tried to pretend they were anything but, this denial only lasted for the first bite. After that, I was sold. I encourage you to do the same.

Protein sources are so much more than the traditional muscle meats and eggs; in fact, liver is one of the most nutritious foods one can eat. Anecdotally, I have seen it help skin and eyesight and raise iron levels. Our baby Aries' first food was a mix of liver and bone marrow, a mix of high-quality protein, fat, and micronutrients (and for the record, she is 85 percent for height and 75 percent for weight, and I am 5'1"!).

In the following pages, you will find delicious recipes that I believe are some of the missing links to health. Understanding the importance of protein, specifically animal-based protein and eating nose-to-tail, can eliminate much of the disease that plagues our society today. *It Takes Guts* is a cookbook I will be recommending to all my patients, as it truly paves the way toward optimal health.

Dr. Gabrielle Lyon

June 10, 2020

INTRODUCTION

" HE WAS **A BOLD MAN** THAT
FIRST ATE AN
OYSTER. "

-JONATHAN SWIFT

I think I was a picky eater at one point; I remember being made to sit at the table as a kid until I finished my meal (although if my memory serves me, it was green beans getting cold on my plate, not liver). But for my entire adult life, I've approached eating as an adventure. I love to try new foods and different cuisines; unique flavors, textures, colors, and combinations fill me with excitement and joy. I'll try anything once—I'm one of those "don't knock it till you try it" kind of people, especially when it comes to food. There's so much deliciousness in the world that it would be a shame to shut yourself off from much of it simply because it's unfamiliar. Sometimes things that "look gross" to the unaccustomed eye taste fantastic, as anyone who's enjoyed a good liver pâté or roasted bone marrow can attest.

Consider one of my absolute favorite foods, lobster. Many of us in North America (and especially on the east coast of Canada, where I'm from) know it to be a delicious and special treat, from the springy, sweet flesh of the tail to the tomalley, the soft, greenish digestive gland found in the body cavity that is considered a delicacy. But people who aren't used to the idea of cracking open giant insects and feasting on their insides might understandably find it terrifying, in the same way that many of us in North America arbitrarily consider eating fried insects, as people do in some Eastern cultures, to be, well, terrifying. Back in the 1800s, prisons on the east coast of North America fed their inmates lobster because it was so abundant, until the criminals complained that it was cruel and inhumane to be forced to eat the bottom-feeding pests. Can you imagine? Those utterly delicious crustaceans are a great illustration that when it comes to food, it's all about perspective, and that having an open mind (and mouth, if I may be so bold) can lead to amazing gustatory experiences.

If I had a dollar for every time someone told me, "I just can't get my head around eating [insert type of organ meat here] because I didn't grow up eating it," I could retire now and live out the rest of my days eating animal hearts on a beach somewhere—but with all due respect, I think it's a bit of a cop-out. I didn't grow up eating organ meat, either; I grew up eating cereal and bread and skim milk and chicken breast, and while I always gravitated toward animal products, I certainly wasn't eating liver or sweetbreads. Look, I know it's pointless to force gizzards on someone who has no interest in them (just ask my mother; as a "recovering vegetarian" and still-reluctant meat-eater, she is continually horrified that she gave birth to someone who gleefully eats brains and tongues), but I do encourage a little adventurousness when you eat. One

bite of something new won't hurt you, and it just might open up a whole new world of pleasure and health. Whether or not the thought of eating organs grosses you out, it's a fact that the organs are generally the most nutrient-dense parts of an animal. So if we can find fun and creative and even subtle ways to enjoy them, we're winning. And by eating the whole animal, we're also honoring and respecting the beings that sacrificed their lives for our dinner plates by ensuring none of it goes to waste.

My hope for this book is to provide an entertaining and user-friendly guide to enjoying some of the more adventurous parts of the animal, as well as understanding the value of whole-animal cooking. I promise the recipes are not complicated, but they *are* delicious. I have no background in cooking or baking, and I did not grow up eating organ meats, so I really mean it when I say that if I can do it, so can you.

This is not me attempting to be humble: despite loving food more than the average person, I've never had a particular passion for the preparing and cooking of said food. I vaguely remember taking a "home economics" class in junior high (I promise I'm not old), which was essentially for the purpose of learning how to cook dinner. The grade I received was something to the effect of "at least you didn't set fire to anything." I'm not writing this cookbook with grand delusions of becoming the next big celebrity chef; I'm writing it because I feel strongly about honoring the animals we're eating and enjoying the full bounty of delicious and healthy options available to us.

During the course of writing, I've become even more excited and empowered to explore the endless possibilities available to us through different cultures, cuisines, and ingredients. Every time I put together a recipe with a new ingredient, successfully develop a dish that seemed more challenging than I was ready for, or make a meal with organ meats that people truly enjoy eating, I feel such a sense of accomplishment, and that's my hope for you, too. I've also enlisted contributions from some of my friends—chefs and recipe developers who are known for their beautiful preparations of nose-to-tail dishes—to make sure both your body and your palate are nourished and satisfied.

Friends, I'm just a food enthusiast whose greatest joy is eating and sharing delicious things. I appreciate your willingness to come along for the ride, because I know it takes guts—literally and figuratively, in this case. As the saying goes, the way you do anything is the way you do everything, and I believe we all should be approaching our plates, and our lives, with a sense of adventure.

HOW TO USE THIS BOOK

Before we go any further, I want to walk you through how this book is organized so that you can access the information you want quickly and easily.

The first chapter of this book, "Let's Talk Offal," should convert you into a willing and optimistic offal eater, if you're not one already. When you learn about all the benefits for your health, the environment, and your wallet, I hope you will be convinced that eating offal makes sense. Besides, not only does offal taste great, but eating it is the right thing to do: if we're going to eat animals, don't we owe it to each animal to make good use of all of it?

Chapter 2, "A Kitchen Primer," breaks down key terms and discusses the different types of offal used in the book, giving information on the health benefits, typical preparations, and sourcing of each type. Two lists round out the chapter: one of key ingredients and the other of the equipment and tools you'll need to make these recipes.

Next come the recipe chapters. As you've probably already gathered, this is not a typical cookbook with typical ingredients, and it's not laid out like a typical cookbook, either. Instead of the more usual organization of recipe by type or category, such as breakfasts, appetizers, and soups, the bulk of the recipes are organized into chapters by "part" (think liver, heart, bones, and so on). If, however, you'd like to access the recipes by basic type or theme, such as breakfasts or soups, simply turn to the general index at the back of the book (beginning on page 261). Whether you're in the mood to make cookies or a stew, you'll find all the applicable recipes listed there.

Finally, although many of the recipes are complete meals on their own, others require a side to make a full meal. For those, I recommend pairings, many of which are found in Chapter 10, "Awfully Good Sides, Snacks, and Sauces." The recipes in this last chapter do not actually contain offal; they are just tasty, healthful, and fun additions that work well with the other recipes or on their own.

Every recipe has an introductory note, many of which give some context for the recipe, telling the story of how it came to be. In the introductions to the contributed recipes, you'll hear about the professional chef or friend who created it, sometimes directly from them! In an unconventional cookbook like this one, I believe the recipe introductions play an extra important role, and I highly recommend you read them before diving into the recipes—whether for inspiration or for guidance. Besides, the only thing better than a delicious meal is a good story to go with it, and I think knowing the background of a dish helps us enjoy it more fully and makes the unfamiliar less scary and more exciting.

To make the recipes as user-friendly as possible, I've included practical information on storage, serving, and substitutions as well as tips and tricks for preparation. You'll also find icons at the tops of the recipes, when applicable, to help you quickly spot which recipes are suited to your skill level—beginner or advanced—and/or the time you have on your hands to spend in the kitchen.

 These recipes are perfect for a beginner cook who has no experience working with offal. These dishes are easy to make and crowd-pleasing—even for organ meat novices!

 These recipes are for the more experienced and adventurous cook. They may take a bit more work in either preparation or sourcing and may use trickier-to-find ingredients.

 Quick and delicious, these recipes take less than thirty minutes to throw together. They are ideal for when you're pressed for time.

Following the recipes, you'll find several helpful resources to enhance your experience with this book. The Suggested Menus section on pages 232 to 235 offers ideas for everyday eating needs—from breakfast through dinner—along with entertaining needs, in case you decide to throw together a dinner party or brunch for friends and family. For an expanded discussion about raising and purchasing good-quality offal, see my interview with Tara Couture that starts on page 236, titled "A Conversation with a Farmer." Finally, at the end of the book, you'll find a short Resources section with helpful guidance on sourcing ingredients and a References section with my suggestions for further reading and research. The indexes at the very back will help you quickly find the perfect recipe, whether you're looking to make liver or bone broth.

Now, let's dig in!

CHAPTER 1

LET'S TALK OFFAL

" THIS MAGICAL, MARVELOUS
FOOD ON OUR PLATE,
THIS SUSTENANCE WE ABSORB, HAS
A STORY TO TELL. IT HAS A JOURNEY. "

-JOEL SALATIN

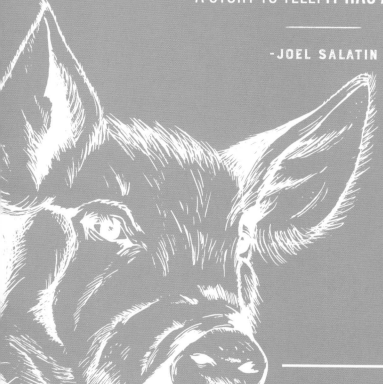

Before we dive deep into the bowels of our favorite animals (very literal, I know; you're going to have to get used to that), I think now is a good time to define some terms. As you try new and sometimes intimidating dishes for the first time—actually, scratch that, when you're doing *anything* for the first time—educating yourself is crucial. The more you know about something, the less scary it is, generally speaking. The more knowledge you have about what you're working with, how to work with it, and why you want to eat it, the better prepared you are to cook and enjoy offal. The more comfortable you get with different parts of the animal, the more you'll see how arbitrary and frankly silly it is to be scared of organ meats, especially if you're already happily eating other parts.

Consider that some edible parts—like testicles, tongue, and brain—are seen as extreme and grotesque by most modern eaters, especially in Western culture. Yet other "atypical" parts, such as bone marrow and even sweetbreads, are sought-after delicacies at some of the best restaurants. Why? Is sucking the goodness out of an animal's bones somehow inherently less gross than eating what's inside its head? It goes to show that what we consider acceptable is really all about perspective, and opening your perspective to new, exciting, and healthy opportunities is a good thing.

So let's get to it, shall we?

WHAT IS OFFAL?

Whatever you do, don't use Dictionary.com to learn what offal is. I did it for you, and the results were pretty disappointing:

offal—**aw**-*fuh* l

noun

—the parts of a butchered animal that are considered inedible by human beings; carrion.

—the parts of a butchered animal removed in dressing; viscera.

—refuse; rubbish; garbage.

Well, if you ask me, that definition is refuse; rubbish; garbage. It's a stereotype that perpetuates the waste and misuse of so many under-appreciated and nutritious animal parts, especially when we're already harvesting the flesh, or the muscle meat, which comprises the cuts we are most used to consuming.

But the plot thickens: if you scroll down the Dictionary.com page, you'll find another definition of offal that reads, "the edible internal parts of an animal, such as the heart, liver, and tongue." That is getting closer but still drastically undersells the wonders that offal can bring to the kitchen and to your palate.

Wikipedia tells us (sorry, but I'm a millennial, and I find my answers online) that offal goes by a number of other names, ranging from more to less scary-sounding—variety meats, pluck, or organ meats—and comprises the internal organs and entrails of a butchered animal. While that description doesn't sound particularly appetizing, technically it is the truth. The Wikipedia entry goes on to describe the somewhat frustrating reality whereby Western culture considers some organ meats to be awful and others to be delicacies deserving of five-star treatment. Wikipedia mentions the prevalence of offal in cuisines around the world, from Scottish haggis (a hearty savory pudding made with oatmeal, onion, suet, liver, heart, and lungs) to Jewish chopped liver to Vietnamese pho (a noodle soup made with veggies and a range of meats, including tendon and tripe; you'll find an awesome version on page 108).

As long as humans have been eating animals (which is to say, since the first humans walked the earth), eating the entire animal has been the M.O.; only recently has it gone out of favor, and even now it's relatively a privileged few in the Western world who consider it taboo. Offal has been a significant part of Traditional Chinese Medicine (TCM) for more than three thousand years, and one of the basic tenets of TCM is that consuming the organ meat of an animal will support the same organ in your own body. I haven't found any definitive evidence that this is the case, but I do know that organ meat contains bioavailable nutrition that is tough to find in such concentrated amounts in other foods and thus can contribute greatly to both specific and general functions within the body. I believe that given its enduring effectiveness, Eastern medicine is an area of study and knowledge that should not be dismissed. I'm grateful for modern medicine, but I'd rather eat real food than take pills.

Just so we're all clear moving forward, as I may use the terms *offal* and *organs* interchangeably: an organ, essentially, is a collection of tissues dedicated to a specific biological function. As you'll see below, things like blood, tendons, and tongue are all considered organs by this definition.

So there you have it: offal, or organ meats—or, if you want to be romantic and Italian with it, *quinto quarto* (the fifth quarter)—is essentially a collection of edible organs and bits and pieces of an animal aside from muscle meat. It is, according to *my* personal definition, "a literal treasure trove of tasty, healthy delights." If you want to add this much more pleasant definition to Wikipedia, feel free—just make sure to credit your girl.

A BREAKDOWN OF THE BENEFITS OF OFFAL

There are so many great reasons to adopt a whole-animal, nose-to-tail approach to eating that they could fill an entire book, but I know you're here for the good stuff: tasty recipes. Still, I believe that understanding why we eat the way we eat is important. Our choices matter, and we should know why particular foods are beneficial for us and how our choices fit into the food industry and the larger community of which we are a part. And look, I get it: when it comes to eating liver and tripe, some of you may still need some convincing, or you may need some words of wisdom to explain to your friends and family why you've gone nose-to-tail. So here is an overview of the reasons I eat this way and encourage others to do so as well.

IT'S SUSTAINABLE

It would be wasteful to buy a large house and use only one or two rooms, right? Or to pick up one of those party bags of chocolate bars, eat only the peanut butter cups, and throw away the rest? Well, the same goes for eating only muscle meat: in a conversation with real-food dietitian, author, and farmer Diana Rodgers, she explained that only 42 percent of harvested cattle is boneless cuts (the meat we would generally pick up at a grocery store); the rest is organs, blood, hide, and bones. Around 25 to 35 percent of the total volume of US beef is edible by-product, which means not leather or bones, but not your typical steak, either—I'm talking about offal. While most of these by-products don't go to waste (they are usually harvested and processed for pet food or exported to other countries that happily consume organ meats), we are essentially bypassing some of the most nutrient-dense food on the planet to eat only the muscle meat, which, nutrition-wise, should be considered the leftovers. Adopting a whole-animal approach reduces waste, and buying from local farms and butchers helps decrease the carbon footprint created when meat is brought to you from far-flung places.

ANIMAL BY-PRODUCTS ARE EVERYWHERE!

It's heartening to know just how little of the animal is wasted during processing and just how important and ubiquitous animal by-products are in all areas of our lives. For your edification, here is an inexhaustive list of everyday products that come from animals and animal production:

- Paintbrushes and makeup brushes are often made from animal hair.
- Shampoo and skincare products often contain animal fat.
- Perfume often contains castoreum, a musk derived from beaver.
- Condoms often contain glycerin, which is made from animal fat.
- Shimmery nail polish and makeup often get their shimmer from powdered fish bones and scales.
- Sports equipment like basketballs and footballs are made from animal hides.
- Industrial lubricants and cleaners often contain beef fat.
- Even medicine like non-synthetic insulin, ointments, and creams contain stearic acid, which is derived from fatty acids from cattle.

Have you heard of regenerative farming? What about the work being done to understand the environmental benefits of letting animals graze in pasture the way their wild ancestors did? Our soil contains less carbon today than it did before people started mass-producing crops, and carbon is what helps plants grow. Allowing animals to graze naturally—that is, to snack here and there and move freely, pooping and trampling plant life as they go, stirring up soil, adding to the nutrients, and never overgrazing in any area—helps add carbon and other nutrients back to the soil, improving air quality, helping plants grow, and allowing the animals to live happier, healthier lives to provide healthier meat for us.

According to Rodgers, much of our land is suitable for grazing and not crops. This is not a zero-sum game, where land that is grazed by animals is being taken away from plant crops. Raising animals on land covered with grass that we can't eat, on land that can't grow crops, only makes sense. To make the land beautiful and green and healthy, you need plants *and* animals to eat, fertilize the soil, and stimulate root growth, which improves water-holding capacity and in turn supports more plant life. Well-tended cattle can actually improve soil health. In fact, says Rodgers, cattle are one of our best chances to reverse desertification, which is what happens when continuous cropping or grazing results in depleted soil nutrients and soil erosion. Properly tended cattle that are "responsibility rotated on pasture" (allowing the pasture to grow and thrive without overgrazing) can maintain a net neutral or even a net gain for carbon sequestration—the removal of carbon dioxide from the atmosphere to slow or reverse carbon dioxide pollution and subsequently slow or reverse the harmful effects of global warming.

These concepts are important for all of us, vegans and meat-eaters and omnivores alike—regardless of whether you enjoy offal—because it's about understanding the impact of the choices we make when we buy certain foods. The more we can contribute to a healthy, natural life cycle for ourselves, animals, and the environment in which we all live, the better off the entire world will be. Minimizing waste and carbon footprint while maximizing the health of the planet and all its inhabitants should be our goals, regardless of the specifics of our diet.

IT'S ETHICAL

My opinion (and you know the saying, opinions are like . . . hearts; we all have one) is this: eating high-quality animal protein is in the best interest of most humans. Sourcing ethically raised and harvested animal protein is in the best interest of humans, animals, and the environment and world in general. If you're going to do something, do it right. Buying local grass-fed or pasture-raised animal products fights inhumane factory farming practices, supports local farmers, mitigates antibiotic usage and thus prevents antibiotic resistance, and helps animals live happy lives.

If you're reading this, you probably eat animals, and if you've accepted that eating animals is a natural part of living, the best way forward is to ensure that the animals you're eating lived a healthy, natural life and were slaughtered humanely. I don't have to remind you that animals eat other animals in nature (often in ways we would consider pretty inhumane) and that "natural death" for animals doesn't usually look like Bambi slipping away quietly in his sleep in a flower-filled meadow at a ripe old age. Death is a part of life; we are a part of the food chain; no matter what you eat, animals will die somewhere along the process. The more we explore it, understand it, and come to terms with it—as uncomfortable as it may be—the better the choices we can make for ourselves, our families, and our community.

Factory farming is bad for everyone; anyone who understands the conditions set by mass factory farming would agree with this, meat-eater or not. The answer, however, is not to turn to mass-produced, chemical-filled, overly processed plant-based products; it's to invest in and seek out foods from local farms that use humane and sustainable practices.

I don't want to reduce this discussion to a "plants versus animals" debate, because that's already been done. It's exhausting, and in my opinion that debate directs criticism in the wrong direction. Some people choose, for personal reasons, to eat an entirely plant-based diet, but most of us in the Western world still choose an omnivorous diet that is made up of both plants and animals. With some mindfulness and attention, we can reduce our carbon footprint by selecting plants and animals that are ethically and locally produced. A 100 percent plant-based diet is not inherently better for the planet; unless you are solely eating plants that you grew in your backyard, many vegan foods are highly processed products that must travel long distances to get to you, and the environmental effects and animal life lost as a result of grain and vegetable monocrops are a significant issue that I won't even get into here.

The point is, all diets require the sacrifice of life: plant life; the lives of smaller insects, rodents, and animals that die in the harvesting of crops; or the lives of animals harvested for their flesh. The sooner we accept that we are a part of the circle of life and that things must die for us to live, the sooner we can focus on causing the least harm to the planet through our actions while supporting a sustainable and healthy diet for ourselves.

Ethical farming practices should be a priority for vegans and meat-eaters alike, considering that all of us are reliant on animal products in some way or another. According to Rodgers, some vegan crops are grown using animal fertilizer, and factory-farmed animal waste can contain antibiotics and other elements we do not wish to have leach into plant foods, so supporting better farm practices will also have a positive effect on those foods. The Western world simply doesn't have the resources to produce the volume of grain and other plant crops needed to meet demand without the use of animal fertilizer, so we're better off improving the quality than fighting against a necessity.

Ideally, your goal should be to minimize waste wherever possible: eat what you buy, purchase only what you'll eat, and compost anything that is left over. Eating ethically also means educating yourself on where your food is coming from and aiming to buy and eat locally and sustainably produced food that does not have to be transported long distances.

No one is perfect all the time, and shaming others (or yourself) for being imperfect is a waste of time that does nothing to solve our problems. The best way forward is to educate yourself, ask questions, and make the best choice available when you can.

IT'S HEALTHY

It's a fact: organ meats like liver, heart, and kidney are nutritional powerhouses, not just for their individual nutrients but for the synergistic effect of consuming these nutrients together. Nutrients like vitamin A, vitamin D, and magnesium work together with other food-based compounds. That's why taking many of these nutrients on their own (in pill form, for example) doesn't have as much of a positive effect on your body. You just absorb nutrients better when they come from whole foods. For example, vitamins A, D, and K are called fat-soluble vitamins because they must be consumed with fat for optimal absorption. You've probably heard that curcumin, the active compound in turmeric, works better in the presence of black pepper—the same goes for many of these animal-derived nutrients.

Another fact: to achieve an optimal nutrition profile from a vegan diet is very difficult and often requires expensive supplementation, tricky manipulation of macros, or, put simply, eating a hell of a lot of veggies to hit your target nutrient intake. Meanwhile, organ meats are so nutrient dense that you can eat very small amounts and get more benefit than you would from nearly any other food on the planet. A few ounces of beef liver contains your daily needs for many nutrients, including iron, copper, zinc, folate, choline, and vitamins A and B12.

Many vitamins and nutrients found in offal, including B6 and folate, support a healthy pregnancy. B vitamins like niacin, riboflavin, and B12 and B6, which are associated with cardio-protective benefits and brain health, are highly concentrated in organ meats. CoQ10 functions as an antioxidant and has been used to prevent and treat certain diseases, support heart health and brain function, and boost energy levels. Guess where you find lots of it? That's right— organ meats. The list goes on, and I'll cover it in more detail in the following chapter, but I hope you're starting to get the picture. If you're thinking about quality over quantity and packing the most nutrition into the most compact and bioavailable container, the answer is organ meats.

And the good news keeps coming: when you eat beef liver, your cells store many of these nutrients, so you don't have to eat liver every day to stay healthy; a couple ounces a week should provide you with your required dose of these vitamins. So even if I can't convince you to love the taste of organ meats, I hope I can help you understand that these are superfoods that can dramatically improve your health and bodily function. If you can't look at liver as a culinary treat, you can at least look at it as one of the most effective supplements on the planet.

It's funny how much fear there is around the safety of eating organ meats in a culture where no one bats an eyelash at energy drinks and candy. Traditional media and medicine tell us that we should eat less meat and fat and that the guts of an animal harbor parasites and disease—but that everything in moderation is okay, including overly processed sugar and chemicals that literally have no nutritional value and are scientifically shown to cause chronic disease and sickness.

It is untrue that organ meats like liver and kidney store and contain toxins as many people believe. Organs like the liver filter toxins, usually moving them to the kidneys, from which they are eventually expelled through the urine. Toxins are removed from a healthy, well-functioning animal's body via these miraculous organs just like they are in ours; eating fresh, healthy organs is the same as eating fresh, healthy muscle meat. If toxins do linger in the body, they are generally stored in fat cells (this goes for us too), which is why it's crucial to source high-quality animal protein that is raised without pesticides or antibiotics, because that's where they'll end up: in your delicious, fatty rib-eye.

Because so much special interest (and money) is involved in promoting corn-, soy-, and wheat-based foods while discouraging the consumption of humanely and sustainably raised animals, it's important to approach this topic with a level head and facts rather than emotion. Perhaps we grew up eating cellophane-wrapped snack cakes and not kidneys, so one of them has a comfortable, nostalgic place in our hearts and the other does not; but if we can look at our food from an objective, purely chemical standpoint, the answer is clear: quality animal foods promote health while processed foods do the opposite.

Many of the studies that established our long-held fear of meat have since been debunked, or at least understood to be misinterpreted or taken out of context. As *New York Times* bestselling author and former research biochemist Robb Wolf asserts, correlation does not necessarily equal causation, and just because something is associated with an outcome does not mean that it caused that outcome. Many of the studies that seem to "prove" meat-eating is unhealthy compare vegetarians with people who follow a "typical Western diet," which we know to be made up of mostly processed foods, grains, and sugar. A person following an omnivorous whole-foods diet would have a food plan much more closely resembling a vegetarian's than a "standard American" eater's. Generally speaking, people who follow a vegetarian diet consider themselves to be more health-conscious; they are much more likely to exercise and eat more vegetables and less processed sugar, and less likely to smoke or drink to excess. All these reasons, plus many others, can contribute to better health outcomes, and interpreting this to mean that the lack of animal protein in their diet is the reason for their improved health is, in essence, negligent. Other

studies have shown that when adjusting for other lifestyle factors (i.e., speaking to healthy meat-eaters and non-meat-eaters), there is generally no significant difference in all-cause mortality for vegetarians and non-vegetarians.

This book is not about turning anyone into a Paleo eater or a carnivore: it's about knowing the truth about what you choose to eat so you can do so with understanding.

IT'S ECONOMICAL

Often, organ meats are less expensive than muscle meats simply because they aren't in high demand. Imagine the nutrient-dense parts being sold for scraps while the basic protein is sold at a premium! Unlike prime cuts of grass-fed beef, grass-fed beef liver and kidney are pretty cheap. A beef tongue can feed a party of six for about ten bucks; chicken hearts are often sold for a few bucks a pound; and you can buy a bag of tasty, protein-packed chicken gizzards that will serve a whole family for less than you'd pay for a fancy salad at your local fast-casual restaurant.

If you want to get the best nutritional bang for your buck with protein, your best bet is to throw some offal in there. Make friends with your local butcher, too; a friend of mine overheard someone in line at the meat counter ask for chicken without the skin—imagine!—so she scooped up the skin for herself, for free.

IT'S FUN (I'M SERIOUS!)

If you can reframe your perceptions of organ meat being "gross" or extreme and see it for what it really is—just a different part of the animal you're already eating, and a much more nutritious part at that—you can start having fun with different recipes and preparations. Anyone who's followed a strict diet or a budget that required them to eat the same boring protein over and over (plain chicken breast or ground turkey, anyone?) can attest that these types of meals are decidedly not fun. But grilled chicken hearts, sliced beef tongue sandwiches, and crispy pigs' ears—now that sounds like a party!

Nose-to-tail eating is also a celebration of culture and history, honoring a time when people were less swayed by grocery store marketing and more driven by instinct, when they hunted and harvested the organ meats for themselves and left the muscle meat to scavengers, when they gave more respect to the time, skill, and labor of providing meals for their families, and when nourishment mattered more than hyperpalatability.

The North American disdain for organ meats is unique; most cultures celebrate offal in their cuisine on some level, and many of these recipes are beloved and time-honored because creating something delicious and nourishing from what many consider to be scraps requires a deeper level of care and creativity. And you don't have to look to the other side of the earth for examples. Indigenous peoples in the Canadian Rockies consume wild moose and caribou year-round. In Canadian Inuit communities, seal hunting is an important cultural experience and a main driver of the economy, including consumption of raw seal heart as well as raw whale blubber and raw caribou. Indigenous peoples learned, simply through experience, that organ meats were superior to muscle meat and had medicinal properties. These hunters often fed muscle meat to the dogs following a hunt, keeping the more nutrient-dense organs for themselves.

In fact, if you care to look, you'll find plenty of pockets throughout North America where people enjoy more adventurous dishes that feature offal. Ever heard of Rocky Mountain oysters? Those are fried bull testicles, and you can get them in the Western United States and Canada. In the South, you can find dishes like boudin (blood sausage), chitterlings (fried or stewed pig intestines), and turkey and chicken giblets (fried heart, liver, and gizzards). In Jewish delis, you'll find plenty of people happily scarfing sliced-tongue sandwiches.

IT'S TASTY (I REALLY MEAN IT)

Don't knock it till you've tried it—that's what I'm always telling my skeptics. While certain organ meats have stronger flavors and unique textures and may never appeal to some people, the same can be said for less controversial foods like tofu and faux-meat products. (Don't even get me started on broccoli—now that's an acquired taste.) I know I'll never win everyone over, but if you're willing to at least try, I think you'll be pleasantly surprised at how delicious, delicate, and decadent offal can be. Eating only muscle meat is like eating cake without the frosting—you're skipping the most fun and flavorful part. Life's too short to skip the frosting, or the offal. So let's dig in!

CHAPTER 2

A KITCHEN PRIMER

" LET **FOOD** BE THY **MEDICINE,**
& MEDICINE
BE THY FOOD."

-HIPPOCRATES

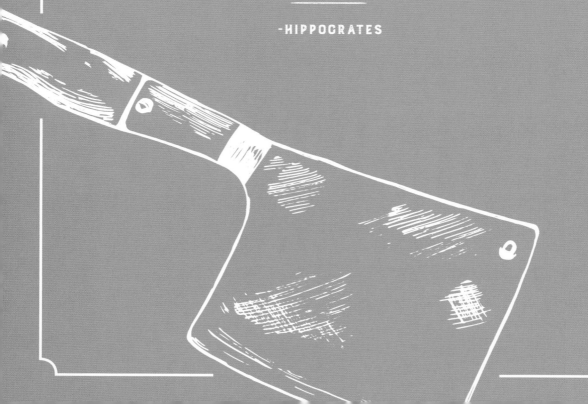

Now that I've explained what offal is and why it's a good idea to eat it, let's talk about how to source organ meats and dig a little deeper into the ingredients you'll be using to make the recipes in the book.

MEAT QUALITY AND SOURCING

First, let's talk a bit about the importance of quality, the terms that are used to define quality, and how to source these ingredients. Whether we're talking about offal, vegetables, or anything else, quality matters, and the more we can learn about the origins of our food, the better decisions we can make.

The United States Department of Agriculture (USDA) defines the term *organic* this way: "Organic is a labeling term that indicates that the food or other agricultural product has been produced through approved methods. The organic standards describe the specific requirements that must be verified by a USDA-accredited certifying agent before products can be labeled USDA organic. Overall, organic operations must demonstrate that they are protecting natural resources, conserving biodiversity, and using only approved substances."

The USDA further asserts that organic livestock must be:

- Produced without genetic engineering, ionizing radiation, or sewage sludge

- Managed in a manner that conserves natural resources and biodiversity

- Raised per the National List of Allowed and Prohibited Substances

- Overseen by a USDA National Organic Program–authorized certifying agent, meeting all USDA organic regulations

- Generally, managed organically from the last third of gestation (mammals) or second day of life (poultry)

- Allowed year-round access to the outdoors except under specific conditions (for example, inclement weather)

- Raised on certified organic land meeting all organic crop production standards

- Raised per animal health and welfare standards

- Fed 100 percent certified organic feed, except for trace minerals and vitamins used to meet the animal's nutritional requirements

- Managed without antibiotics, added growth hormones, mammalian or avian by-products, or other prohibited feed ingredients (for example, urea, manure, or arsenic compounds)

If you'd like, you can head to the USDA website to read a number of lengthy, confusing, and relatively dry PDFs about "Organic Practices," "Organic Livestock Requirements," handling and labeling standards, and so on, so I won't regurgitate that information here.

Although I know it's problematic to generalize things that just aren't simple, ultimately organic meat comes from farms that use methods of production that involve no pesticides, fertilizers, GMOs, antibiotics, or growth hormones and work to meet the health and other needs of livestock by providing as close to a natural environment as possible. It also means working on maintaining or enhancing the health, vitality, and biodiversity of the soil and the local ecology while promoting each animal's welfare up to and including its "last day."

The process for USDA certification involves five steps, which include developing and implementing an organic system plan outlining how the farm will comply with USDA regulations and then having that plan and system inspected and reviewed. Just because a farm isn't certified organic, however, does not mean that it isn't employing organic and ethical farming practices. Due to costs associated with official certification, many farmers choose not to pursue the label even though they follow organic practices. That's why it's important to know where your food is coming from and to ask questions of your local farmer, butcher, or other provider.

Diana Rodgers says that her working organic farm in Massachusetts doesn't even label its animals as grass-fed even though they are. "We just have a transparent operation," she says, where members can come to the farm and see for themselves how the animals are raised and fed. "I recommend people visit the farm [where their meat comes from] if they can," she says. "It's easy to look around and see if the animals are living good lives."

Grass-fed means only that an animal ate grass at some point during its life cycle, not that it exclusively ate grass. *Grass-finished* means that it ate grass throughout its life cycle. Same goes for the grain-based definitions. All cattle eat grass, but only some eat it exclusively.

The grain-finishing process makes it possible to fatten cattle faster and get them to market sooner (which should make us all think twice the next time we chow down on processed "whole-grain" snacks) and is common practice both in large-scale industrial operations and on local farms. It's worth noting that there is no significant evidence that grass-finished meat is across-the-board healthier, more natural, more sustainable, or morally "better"; many small farmers and producers grain-finish their beef for fattier, more marbled steaks, so you can buy locally and sustainably sourced grain-finished beef.

Whether you are eating grass-fed or grain-fed or -finished meat, there are ways to ensure that it's being done at the highest quality possible. Is the grain grown locally? Do the animals regularly move to different pasture areas so they aren't overgrazing? A concentrated animal feedlot operation where thousands of head of cattle spend miserable lives isn't going to produce high-quality meat.

While there may be nothing necessarily bad or harmful about grain finishing, it does change the composition and flavor of the muscle meat. Grass-finished beef tends to be significantly leaner, with less fat marbling and a darker color. Because it has less fat, you run the risk of a tough, overly chewy product if you don't pay close attention as you cook it. You may want to use more fat when cooking grass-finished meat. Leaner, more "grassy-tasting" meat isn't better or worse; it just has to be approached differently. Some steak-eating connoisseurs describe grass-fed beef as tasting somewhat gamier or earthier, while grain-fed steak has a milder, more "traditional" taste—meaning the taste most of us in the Western world are used to.

As terms like *grass-fed* become marketing tools and selling points, it of course follows that beef labeled this way is more expensive. Marketing is certainly one reason, as well as some slim available data that it may be a slightly healthier option. More practically, grass-fed beef costs more because it takes longer to fatten a cow for slaughter using only grass than using other feed like grain and corn, driving up costs for the producers. (Again, imagine you want to bulk up a little—are you going to go with salads or cornbread?) And because even slaughter-weight grass-fed cows tend to be smaller than corn-fed ones, farmers get less bang for their buck, also driving up the price to make all the work worth their while.

There is research indicating that mostly grass-fed animals are healthier than mostly grain-fed ones, although the difference isn't terribly significant—certainly not enough to forgo meat altogether if you don't have access to grass-fed or grass-finished beef. The real difference lies in the environmental impact. Feeding cattle mostly or exclusively grass, on properly grazed and maintained pastures, makes farmers less reliant on processed feeds, reducing the carbon footprint involved in the production of beef.

GETTING THE GOOD STUFF

I understand as well as anyone that finding the specialty items required for the recipes in this book can take a little extra work. I know this because I spent months researching, seeking, and sometimes failing to find good-quality sources in order to put these recipes together. While you might be surprised by how easy it is to acquire bone marrow or chicken hearts, for example (because they're almost always at the butcher counter; you just skipped right over them), it's not always easy to track down local, fresh tripe, tongue, or sweetbreads.

Why is offal sometimes hard to find? It used to be that when an animal was slaughtered, all the meat—including the organs—was harvested and eaten. It's really only recently that organ meat has become a specialty item. When industrialized farming began to take hold in the late eighteenth century, commercial processing techniques and slaughterhouses proliferated. Offal can be delicate, and thus difficult to store, keep fresh, and transport, so it's easier for commercial processors to sell these pieces for use in products like pet food, or to throw them out. As a result, muscle meat became more common and inexpensive. At the same time, small specialty butcher shops that provided fresh local meat—as well as individualized service and advice on how to cook different cuts—went out of business in favor of larger chain grocery stores offering cheaper, more widely available "basic" cuts, and the appreciation for organ meats declined. These days, many organs are exported to Mexico, South America, and Asia—places that still enjoy more traditional foods like organ meats. In essence, we're exporting the most nutritious parts of the animals and keeping the leftovers for ourselves. Fortunately, the desire for offal is slowly starting to return.

Just as we should always strive to source the highest quality organic protein, the same goes for organs and offal as well. The healthier the animal, the healthier the organ or offal. The most pressing question is whether the meat was raised locally and in a sustainable way.

The best source for organ meats and offal is local farms; you want the freshest product possible, from local, well-raised animals, raised by farmers who can speak to their farming and harvesting practices. (As I mentioned previously, I conducted an interview with just such a farmer, Tara Couture, and you can read an excerpt from that interview beginning on page 236.) You should feel empowered to ask whether the animals are grass-fed or -finished, raised on rotated pasture, and not given grains or antibiotics.

Establishing relationships with local butchers and butcher shops is another great option, as they are more likely to know the origins of their meat and can give you more information about the product than a large chain grocery store with a meat counter. The great thing about a butcher is that you can request specialty items and maybe even get certain products extremely cheap or even free, simply because the pieces are there and no one else wants them!

You can probably find chicken hearts and livers, and maybe even kidneys or gizzards, at your local grocery store.

Finally, there are a number of online purveyors focused on shipping high-quality frozen meat across the United States and Canada to people who don't have access to local farms; more information on some of these companies is available in the Resources section on page 251.

Ultimately, you can make your own choice based on flavor, price, and availability. Eating, like most decisions in life, is about making the best of what's available to you and weighing your options without getting mired down in perfectionism or paralysis by analysis. You always have a choice, and usually a better one can be made with a little mindfulness and research. As Rodgers says, you should aim for the "healthiest, happiest, freshest animals you can access," but remember that "feedlot beef is still better than a Twinkie."

LET'S TALK "SPECIALTY PARTS": FROM HEAD TO TAIL

Now, let's take this a step further and discuss the unique aspects, applications, and nutritional profiles of some of the special ingredients used in this book.

This is not an exhaustive list of all the offal that is used in these recipes; ingredients that are used just once, such as oxtail, are discussed within the context of their recipe. Nor is it an exhaustive list of all the offal that is available to the most resourceful consumers; as I've mentioned before, I'm not a trained chef, and truthfully, some ingredients are beyond my scope in terms of recipe development, which is why you won't see lung, penis, or spleen recipes in this book. (Stay tuned for *It Takes Guts, Part 2: More Guts!*) I encourage you to do your own research. In the spirit of trying new things, I certainly would not turn down a delicious spleen dish if you offered me one. But for the purposes of this book, I am going to outline only the offal ingredients you'll be using in these recipes.

BLOOD

Many people don't know that blood is technically an organ. Pumped by the heart and transported via the veins and arteries, blood carries nourishment throughout the body. It is colored by hemoglobin, a component of red blood cells that bonds with oxygen to carry it throughout the body and removes the carbon dioxide that results from metabolism. Blood from a cow, pig, duck, or chicken is often used to thicken and color stews and soups and to add depth and richness to sausages and even desserts, like my take on Italian *sanguinaccio dolce* (sweet blood pudding) on page 188. (Even if you never make the recipe, you have to read my story about the experience of sourcing pig's blood for the first time!) If the dish is done well, you'll taste an added depth and richness without feeling like a vampire.

Blood is rich in protein, minerals, vitamin D, and (unsurprisingly) iron. In these recipes, it acts as a supporting ingredient that brings out other flavors rather than giving a dish the strong, metallic flavor you might expect. If you are able to source fresh blood, it will have a rich, deep red color (you know, the color of blood) and won't have an overpowering smell—perhaps a bit of a mineral, ironlike aroma. If it is fresh, it will coagulate quickly. Frozen blood may be easier to source (make sure that it was frozen at the peak of freshness); when thawed, it has the same look and feel as fresh. Some specialty markets offer coagulated blood cubes for use in cooking, and others sell freeze-dried blood powder, but freshness is harder to discern in these products, and the taste won't be as deep and rich.

Blood sausage, while intimidating, is one of the richest, most decadent meat dishes I've ever had the good fortune of trying; check out my recipe on page 166. It's a strong flavor for sure, deep and salty, but if you're already a meat-eater, you may be surprised at how quickly you develop a taste for it. Black pudding, well known in places like Scotland, Spain *(morcilla),* and France *(boudin noir),* was developed out of necessity, when folks had no choice but to use every part of the animal—and come up with creative ways to make use of the ingredients right away since they didn't have refrigeration. Enterprising eaters would slaughter an animal and immediately mix the blood with fat, oats, and other spices; pack it into an intestinal casing; and boil it. Luckily for them, that mixture somehow turned out pretty tasty!

The Maasai, a pastoral tribe living in Kenya and northern Tanzania, enjoy a traditional diet consisting largely of cow milk, meat (raw and cooked), and sometimes blood. The tribespeople get blood from their cattle by puncturing the jugular vein in a way that allows them to repeatedly harvest from the animal without killing it. (Talk about a sustainable food source.) Their fat and cholesterol consumption is very high by Western standards, but the Maasai are much slimmer than your typical American and largely free of chronic lifestyle diseases like heart disease and high blood pressure. I'm not telling you to start using your local farm as a continuous nutrition fountain; I'm just using this example to show that there is plenty of precedent for people to incorporate blood into their diet—and they seem to both enjoy it and thrive on it.

It is possible to overdose on iron, resulting in iron toxicity, although this is more commonly a result of taking too many iron supplement pills; most people aren't going to eat too much iron from whole-food sources. So, while there may be individual cases where eating iron-rich foods is a bad idea, for the majority of us, a slice of boudin every now and then has only benefits—and yummy ones.

BONES: MARROW, COLLAGEN, AND GELATIN

Marrow is the spongy tissue found inside bones. This material generates red and white blood cells, is a part of the immune system, and is largely fat. It has a jellylike consistency and, when roasted, a fatty, buttery taste and mouthfeel. I'm going to go out on a limb here and say that marrow is universally delicious, and if you don't agree, you're crazy. (If you don't believe me, give the Super Sexy Bone Marrow recipe on page 66 a try. It's barely a recipe because it's so easy to do, and I'm confident you'll enjoy it!)

For whatever reason, bone marrow tends to be one of the more readily accepted specialty items found on fine-dining and trendy menus; it's long been enjoyed all over the world. Special spoons were even developed in eighteenth-century France and England for the sole purpose of scooping bone marrow. It's used in a number of cuisines to thicken soups and stocks and can be whipped into butter for an ultra-decadent topping for warm, crusty bread. (Drooling yet? Check out my Whipped Bone Marrow Butter recipe on page 68.)

This delicacy is chock-full of amino acids, collagen, vitamins, and minerals that support bone and skin health as well as fight inflammation. Bone marrow includes collagen, but not all collagen is bone marrow. Collagen (usually available in the form of unflavored powdered collagen peptides) is a protein consisting of amino acids, and it's a structural building block for the connective tissues of the body, like tendons and ligaments, as well as skin, hair, and the gut lining. One great way to get all the benefits of collagen and bone marrow is bone broth; I have a number of recipes in the chapter on bones, starting on page 50, because you can make bone broth with any leftover bones you have on hand, and they all impart a different flavor. From turkey to chicken to wild game and beyond, the best-quality bones yield a rich, tongue-coating, and savory broth that is warm, filling, rich in nutrients, and a great additive to your cooking. (I cook rice in bone broth, for example, to impart a tasty flavor and more nutrients to my starchy side dish.)

You might be thinking: collagen is pretty mainstream and not that gross or scary, so why is it included here? Well, collagen is usually sourced from cows or fish and is made from processed and powdered bovine hide or fish scales, where the collagen is the most concentrated. In most cases, these materials are essentially boiled down into a stew and then sprayed through a high-pressure nozzle into a heat tunnel. The nozzle vaporizes the mixture into droplets that are instantly dried into powder particles. The result is essentially an air-dried, flavorless powder that's high in collagen protein. So, when you're spooning the collagen powder into your coffee or baking, you're getting an amino acid and protein boost from powdered bovine hide or fish scales.

Since it's pretty difficult to come up with offal-based desserts, I have included a bunch of collagen-based ones instead, like my Mint Chocolate Coconut Collagen Cups on page 184. Collagen powder is one of my favorite and most-used supplements, although it's really more of a food product. I get plenty of collagen from my real-food diet, which includes generous amounts of skin-on fish, chicken, pork, and bone broth, but I have noticed that when I incorporate one serving of collagen into my daily routine consistently for a few weeks, my hair and skin look better, my digestion is amazing, and my fingernails grow like Wolverine's (but, like, cuter).

I also use grass-fed gelatin in a number of recipes. Gelatin is simply a more processed version of collagen powder, heated in a way that allows it to absorb water and become thick and sticky (rather than dissolving like collagen powder does); it is responsible for thickening soups, puddings, and Jell-O, among other dishes. Like collagen powder, it is a by-product of processing animal bones, skin, and cartilage to access all the health-promoting amino acids that assist in a properly functioning digestive system as well as support the building blocks of healthy and vibrant hair, skin, and nails. Finding fun ways to incorporate more grass-fed gelatin in your life is a great idea—think gummies, like the tart cherry ones on page 200.

BRAIN

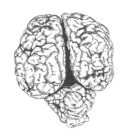

Eat brain to support your own brain function, as some ancestral wisdom goes—and it turns out, our ancestors may have been on to something. While you may not be taking on the intelligence of the pig or lamb whose brain you're eating (probably a good thing), a healthy animal brain, which is (like yours) about 60 percent fat, is a great source of bioavailable omega-3 fatty acids. Omega-3 supports brain function, among many other benefits. The best news of all is that brain has a mild, delicious flavor—if you like a decadent, rich, creamy pâté, you'll love some brain on your plate. A fresh brain is soft and wobbly and creamy pinkish-white in color; it has that tell-tale lobed appearance that makes the organ so distinctive, is delicate to the touch, and has no strong odor.

Most brain recipes use pig, sheep, lamb, veal, or cow organs. The use of this ingredient is considered taboo in many circles, as eating diseased brains has been known to result in awful neurodegenerative diseases like mad cow (which doesn't affect humans but in very rare cases can cause a variant called Creutzfeldt-Jakob that can be fatal) or scrapie, but these maladies are pretty rare these days; just like any meat you buy, you should take care to get fresh, local, well-raised product. Once you get past the squeamishness, you'll be pleasantly surprised at how easy brain is to cook. Since it's nice and fatty, you can sauté or pan-fry it and achieve a nice crusty exterior without breading and a creamy, custard-like interior. It goes well with scrambled eggs (see page 90) due to its mild flavor and similar consistency. Brain can be a special treat on the menus of biohackers, Paleo eaters, and keto dieters alike due to its nutrient density and high fat content.

GIZZARDS

Here's something I didn't know until I researched it—gizzards are nutritional powerhouses! In fact, I'd already eaten gizzards before I knew how nutritious they are and the role they play. The gizzard is an organ found in the digestive systems of some animals, like chickens and fish (but not humans). It's used to grind food rather than let it slosh around in stomach acids like it does in humans. Technically speaking, the gizzard is a type of stomach. Often, gizzards contain grit to aid in the grinding action, so it's important to remove that stuff before you cook them. Gizzards aren't too intimating to look at or handle: they're like little bits of dark meat with some visible outer fat or connective tissue that you can remove or cut away. Most of the time, when you purchase gizzards, they will already be prepared for you: that is, cut open and cleaned out of the inner grit. They should be a deep, rich red color, similar to liver, with a clean, meaty smell.

This organ is high in selenium and pretty high in protein; a modest 4-ounce serving contains around 30 grams of protein. When prepared properly, gizzards are juicy and delicious. So, for all you meatheads and bodybuilders out there looking to get jacked and support muscle growth, get yourself some gizzards!

Gizzards are muscular organs, so they take a bit more care and cooking to ensure that they're tender and pleasantly chewy. They are often fried or baked. The ones you're most likely to come across in grocery stores and in restaurants are from turkeys or chickens.

HEART

Heart is an all-around winner and a surprisingly great starting point for people just getting comfortable with the whole-animal approach to eating. The heart, as I'm sure you know, circulates blood. It is the strongest and most fibrous muscle in the body, which means that it can be tough or chewy. But trust me, as someone who's eaten a lot of hearts (just ask my ex-boyfriends), when I say that if prepared properly, heart is tender and delicious. It's not quite as nutritionally powerful as liver (see page 37), but it's a whole lot easier to prepare and eat.

Heart is both an organ and a muscle, so it's mild in flavor and has a familiar beefy texture. It also has the highest amount of the powerful antioxidant CoQ10 of any offal, as well as plenty of vitamin B12, riboflavin, niacin, iron, phosphorus, copper, and selenium. It's high in protein and relatively low in fat. Fresh hearts are a rich red color, firm to the touch like most muscle meat, with some outer fat, arteries, and veins that you can cut away. Heart is rich in minerals and may have a stronger meaty smell than some other muscle meat, but the odor shouldn't be overpowering.

Heart is a popular meat in cuisines and dishes around the world, from South American street food to high-end Japanese restaurant dishes and beyond. It is often grilled on skewers. I've tried cow, bison, buffalo, deer, lamb, elk, and chicken hearts, and all are uniquely delicious.

KIDNEY

The kidneys filter blood, remove waste, and help maintain the ideal balance of nutrients in the circulatory system; animals typically have two of them. The kidneys also make urine, which is why many people wrinkle their noses at the idea of eating them. Eating something that smells like, and once contained, pee is a tough sell! (I know I'm talking semantics here, but it's actually the bladder that stores urine, not the kidneys.)

Eating kidney is a concept you may need a bit of time to wrap your head around, but a serving of cow kidney has more than *five times* the amount of vitamin B12 you need each day, as well as almost twice the riboflavin. It also contains 228 percent of the daily recommended value for selenium, an antioxidant mineral required for immune health, sex hormone production, and kidney function (so, good news, maybe you don't have to eat the whole kidney). This trace mineral is associated with a number of powerful health benefits, including the prevention of certain types of cancer, decreased oxidative stress, and enhanced immune function. Here I am again, showing that perhaps eating the organ supports that organ in your own body. Food is magic!

Since kidneys are busy filtering organs, it is crucial to prepare them properly for cooking, which includes removing the membrane surrounding the kidney and any excess fat, rinsing thoroughly, and soaking in cold water or milk for at least two hours. Soaking kidneys is said to help remove any lingering blood or other impurities and also remove some of the acidity, giving the organs a milder flavor.

Some animal kidneys, like lamb, are smooth and bean-shaped (you guessed it, like kidney beans), while larger kidneys from bison, buffalo, and cow are large, lobed organs; all have the same shiny red color. The raw organ should not smell strongly of ammonia, but when cooked it will have a strong odor and flavor, which is part of this particular organ's appeal for many eaters. The scent and flavor can be reduced, but kidney will always be one of the stronger-tasting organs.

Despite all this work, kidneys are a popular food in many parts of Europe, including England and France (where they're often masked in rich sauces). You may also find them stir-fried in some Asian cuisines. They add a meaty texture and taste to a dish.

LIVER

Liver, for a lot of people, is the big show when it comes to organ meats. It's the one most talked about for its health benefits and . . . well, challenging taste. While liver certainly has a stronger flavor and a more unique texture than muscle meat, I'd argue that most meat-eaters who haven't enjoyed liver just haven't found the right recipe yet.

First, let me put your mind at ease and bust some myths about the "cleanliness" of this organ: the functions of the liver are to regulate cholesterol levels, aid in digestion, and help clear toxins from the body. That doesn't mean that it stores those toxins within itself. Toxins are "methylated," or detoxified, in the liver; the toxins are actually stored in fat cells. This may mean that you have to be more careful about where you're sourcing your fatty cuts of meat than about where the liver you buy is coming from, although you always should aim to source the best-quality meats.

Whether or not you can get behind the taste of liver, there's no denying that it is a nutritional powerhouse; many nutrition experts claim that liver is, pound for pound, the most nutritionally dense food on the planet. Beef liver, for example, contains fifty times as much vitamin B12 as beef steak and more folate and B vitamins than any other food; it's also high in vitamin A, choline, copper, iron, and zinc. A few ounces of chicken liver contain more than double the daily recommended value of vitamins A and B12 and generally supply more than 100 percent of the folate and riboflavin that the average person needs each day. Liver also contains high amounts of vitamin B6, copper, iron, niacin, pantothenic acid, phosphorus, and selenium. It is the best source of copper, CoQ10, and vitamin A (or retinol) for eye and immune health. Quite simply, ounce for ounce, and regardless of the type of liver—beef, pork, chicken, and so on—this organ packs more nutrients than virtually any other food. Perhaps most importantly, you don't have to eat liver every day to reap the rewards—a couple ounces per week should be more than enough.

You may want to consider starting with chicken or duck liver (see my popular Chicken Liver Mousse recipe on page 126) and then move on to calf, goat, and lamb liver before you go all-in on liver from larger animals like cows; the livers of smaller animals are relatively more delicate and milder tasting. Fresh liver has a deep red color; a smooth, firm-yet-puddinglike feel; and an iron-rich smell. The naturally creamy texture of liver lends itself well to whipped mousse and pâté, which tend to be more palatable. It is also a common practice to mix small amounts of liver into other dishes, like mixing it with ground beef for burgers or meatballs (as in the recipes on pages 132 and 134) as a way to boost nutrition without altering the familiar taste of your favorite meals. In some cultures, liver is eaten raw; fish liver sashimi is popular in Japan, for example.

SKIN

Yup, skin is an organ, and a very important one. It's the largest organ (by weight) of most animals. As with most things, like a good cookie or my sleep routine, it's more complicated than it appears.

Skin has three layers: the epidermis, dermis, and hypodermis, the latter being mostly fat. It acts as a protective layer for the animal and helps regulate body temperature. Skin can be eaten and enjoyed attached to the underlying flesh and fat, like with a delicious roast chicken or pork belly; on its own, as in my Sweet Cinnamon Chicharrones on page 186; or crisped up and used as a flavor and texture enhancer, like the Crispy Salmon Skin Salad on page 172. The skin is often where the flavor, texture, and nutrition are the most concentrated. I've always said to anyone who will listen (although admittedly, no one has ever asked) that there are two types of people: those who eat meat with the skin on and those who are wrong. Seriously, though, if you're skipping the skin, you're missing out on lots of healthy fats and one of the most delicious parts of the animal.

Ask your butcher to provide you with a pound or so of fresh, cleaned pork skin or the skin of a chicken carcass (since many people request their chickens without skin, that delicious part goes to waste). Fresh skins have no smell, and of course have a different texture or feel depending on the animal: chicken skin is thin, mostly fat, and crisps up quickly, whereas pork skin is much thicker.

SWEETBREADS

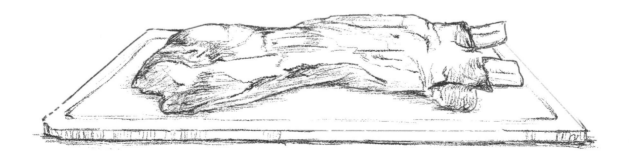

I think I like sweetbreads mostly for the name, but you probably already know that sweetbreads aren't sweet or made of bread—they're glands, from the thymus and pancreas, usually sourced from calves or lambs. Sometimes testicles are lumped into this category as well; all glands look the same to some people, what can I say? Sweetbreads are high in dietary cholesterol (which shouldn't be a problem for most people—after all, our brains run on cholesterol—but worth noting in case cholesterol is something you need to avoid) and vitamin C. Similar to brain, sweetbreads are soft, delicate, and light pink in color, with a lobed, veined appearance; they have no odor. Once cooked, they firm up but retain a creamy bite that makes them an excellent candidate for breading and frying, like my recipe on page 148.

While they may not be a nutritional heavyweight like liver, sweetbreads are a lot easier to swallow, literally, for most people and may be a good "gateway organ" to get you comfortable with some of the more adventurous cuts on this list. These mild and tasty nuggets lend themselves well to frying, sautéing, and even grilling. (You can't go wrong with the recipe for Grilled Sweetbread Tacos on page 144, contributed by chef Nikki DeGidio.) Like bone marrow, you're more likely to see fried or grilled sweetbreads on a menu than most other specialty meats.

TONGUE

I'm going to be honest with you upfront, because that's what this book is about. Tongue is a bit more work for less reward, nutritionally speaking—but the good news is, it's muscle meat, so once you get past the "ew, it's a tongue" reaction, you'll realize that it's delicious. It may be one of the scarier organs to prepare (because it, you know, looks like a tongue), but the taste is mild and the texture is tender. It's also a great source of vitamin B12, niacin, riboflavin, and zinc, important nutrients in which too many of us are chronically deficient. Different animal tongues vary slightly in appearance, but a fresh tongue will be thick, firm, and odorless and will have a clean but obvious tonguelike outer skin with visible taste buds.

Preparing tongue from scratch is not for the faint of heart; peeling the outer layer (the part with the taste buds) off of a footlong cow tongue is pretty grisly, and I say this from vivid and repeated experience. But let's not disrespect this important and delicious gift! Without our tongues, we wouldn't be able to talk or taste. It's a versatile muscle that is delicious prepared in a number of ways: cooked and sliced in a sandwich, the way it's been enjoyed forever in Jewish delis; slow-cooked and shredded in tacos (see page 82), like in any good Mexican food spot; thinly sliced on a charcuterie plate with some peppery mustard; jellied; stir-fried; and the list goes on. Cooking time varies for this cut, as you'll see in the recipes; generally, for a beef tongue, you can cook it in a pot on the stovetop over medium heat for about 4 hours or in a slow cooker on low for up to 8 hours. The former is faster, while the latter requires less attention; either way, you simply cook the tongue until the outer skin separates from the flesh and a fork penetrates the meat easily. Both cooking methods result in a tender, delicious piece of meat.

My favorite tongues (what a weird phrase) come from larger animals like bison and cows, because you get a good amount of meat for a great price. You'll often find duck tongues in Chinese cuisine—but watch out, they have bones in them!

TRIPE

Tripe generally refers to the stomach lining, usually from a cow. There are a few different forms, like honeycomb tripe (named for its distinctly shaped texture) and small intestine. This organ is rich in selenium, vitamin B12, and zinc but is more often included in recipes for its unique texture than its health benefits.

Tripe gets a bad rap for tasting gamey or, worse, reminiscent of its contents, when it's usually the preparation that's to blame; you have to ensure that intestines and stomach lining are carefully cleaned and soaked, after which they take on a relatively neutral flavor that works well in soups and stews (although it should be noted that in some cultures, people prefer not to clean their tripe too much, resulting in a much funkier dish; to each their own!). When you purchase tripe from a butcher or grocery, it often will have been thoroughly cleaned for you, free of debris or membranes: it will be white or off-white and have a thick, rubbery texture that softens when you cook it. When properly cleaned, raw tripe should not have a strong smell.

You'll find tripe in Latin soups and stews like *menudo* and *mondongo,* in Chinese stir-fry dishes, and in African stews. Tripe is also great braised and grilled, but you have to be careful not to overdo it, or you will end up with rubbery meat.

YOUR FRIDGE AND PANTRY: OTHER INGREDIENTS YOU'LL NEED

Now that we've gotten to know the stars of the show, let's go over some other essential ingredients you'll need for this book, and for cooking in general. This is not an exhaustive list, but in my opinion it's a great starting point. These ingredients will come in handy for most recipes and are always good to have around.

- **Butter and/or ghee, unsalted, grass-fed**

- **Coconut oil, cold-pressed, organic**

- **Olive oil, extra-virgin.** When buying olive oil, you want cold-pressed, extra-virgin olive oil in a dark glass bottle. Look for a harvest date on the label. You want to consume your olive oil within a year of harvest, and ideally within a few months; olive oil is not like wine and does not get better with age—you want it as fresh as possible! If you take a sip of your olive oil and get a little peppery kick at the end, you know it's fresh.

- **Citrus fruits.** Grapefruit, lemons, limes, and blood oranges are my favorites, but you can go with any citrus you like.

- **Fresh garlic, ginger, and onions**

- **Fresh herbs.** I use a lot of basil, dill, mint, parsley, rosemary, thyme, but use whatever suits your taste buds.

- **Chocolate.** I personally don't prefer super dark chocolate; I think something in the 75 percent cacao range is ideal for most recipes and taste buds. There are a bunch of brands of dairy-free chocolate with just a few ingredients like coconut sugar, cocoa butter, and cacao that are fantastic. For white chocolate, you want to find a product that contains at least 20 percent cocoa butter (if you read carefully, many options out there are labeled something like "white baking chips" and contain little to no cocoa butter—they're mostly sugar and oil and won't taste as good!).

- **Collagen powder and gelatin, unflavored, grass-fed** (for desserts, soups, and smoothies)

- **Gluten-free flours.** I generally follow a Paleo-style diet, which eliminates grains, so I tend to work with almond and coconut flours or the Paleo flour mixes that combine different grain-free flours and are easy to swap in for all-purpose flour without adjusting recipes.

- **Ground beef and organ meat mixture.** This comes preground, requiring no prep. It is available online from quality meat purveyors (see page 251). Alternatively, most butcher shops will be able to prepare this for you, and generally they use (or you can request) a 4:1 ratio of ground beef to ground organs. You can request any combination of liver, heart, or kidney; using this ratio, the organ used shouldn't really make a difference in how you use or cook the meat, and won't significantly affect the taste of the meat either. You can also make it homemade if you prefer (see the sidebar on the following page).

- **Nuts and seeds.** Cashews, macadamia nuts, pecans, and sunflower seeds are my favorites, but there are plenty of different kinds out there that you can add to recipes for added fat, flavor, and texture.

- **Sea salt, coarse and fine grain.** In some recipes, a coarser salt is ideal for texture and finishing, while in others you want the salt to disappear and work mostly to enhance other flavors.

- **Spices.** I personally can't go a day without cinnamon or garlic powder, but black pepper, cayenne pepper, cumin, oregano, paprika, turmeric, and other spices are used in these recipes as well.

- **Vinegars** (apple cider, balsamic, and red wine)

HOW TO MAKE GROUND BEEF AND ORGAN MEAT MIXTURE

If you prefer to make this at home, you can purchase fresh or frozen organ meat, thaw the meat in the fridge, if frozen, and combine a ratio of 4:1 ground beef to organ meat (for example, 1 pound of ground beef to ¼ pound of heart) in a food processor until mixed. You will want to add the organ meat, roughly chopped, to the processor first and pulse a few times until it is broken down into pieces similar in size to the ground beef. (In the case of liver, be careful not to overprocess it; because of its creamier texture, it will become pastelike if overmixed. Don't worry, once it's pulsed into smaller chunks, it will mix in fine with the rest of the meat!) Next, add the ground beef and pulse just enough to mix the beef and organ meat together; overprocessing the ground meat can make it tough.

Pro tip: *If you're really worried about an "organ meat" taste, I suggest using heart, which is a muscle meat and not strong tasting, or chicken liver, which is the mildest-tasting animal liver. You can also ask your butcher to premix organ meat into your ground beef for you.*

YOUR TOOLBOX: THE EQUIPMENT YOU'LL NEED

It's just another misconception that preparing and cooking organ meats requires rare or special equipment. You may be pleasantly surprised to learn that you probably already have nearly all the equipment you need to make any of the recipes in this book. Most of the tools listed below are pretty standard kitchen items and will come in handy for the recipes in this book as well as most other recipes out there.

- **Air fryer.** It makes so many recipes faster and easier! I use this small appliance to make three recipes in this book—Chicken Skin Chips (page 170), Plantain Chips (page 214), and Sweet Cinnamon Chicharrones (page 186)—but find it very useful when reheating leftover crispy foods. It perfectly (and quickly) recrisps them while reheating them.

- **Baking pan,** 8-inch square

- **Cake pan,** 9-inch round

- **Cast-iron skillet,** 12-inch. You can use any type of skillet you have to make the recipes in this book, but I recommend a cast-iron skillet for many reasons: it's durable, lasting longer than cookware made of other material when properly maintained; it's versatile (it can go from stovetop to oven and back); it holds heat extremely well; and it's viewed as a healthier alternative to coated nonstick pans.

- **Cheesecloth**

- **Chef's knife and paring knife** (sharp ones, along with a knife sharpener)

- **Cutting board**

- **Dutch oven** or other heavy-bottomed stew pot, 6 quarts

- **Food processor** (7 cups or larger) **and/or blender** (60 ounces or larger). In most of the recipes, either of these two appliances can be used. The ideal choice for the job is always listed first; sometimes the job requires a high-powered blender, and when one is needed, I have noted that.

- **Glass jars and airtight storage containers,** various sizes

- **Hand mixer or stand mixer**

- **Immersion blender**

- **Loaf pans,** 8½ by 4½ inches and 9 by 5 inches

- **Measuring spoons and measuring cups**

- **Meat grinder with sausage attachment.** If you'd like to delve into making homemade sausage, meatballs, or burgers—all effective and tasty ways to "hide" offal—this is a great tool to invest in, but it's not necessary; many butcher shops will grind meat for you. I use it to make Pork Heart Sausage Sheet Pan Dinner (page 96).

- **Mixing bowls,** various sizes

- **Parchment paper**

- **Rimmed baking sheet,** 18 by 13 by 1 inch

- **Saucepans,** 1½, 2, and 3 quarts

- **Slow cooker or Instant Pot,** 6 quarts

- **Spatulas,** metal and silicone

- **Whisk,** 12 inches

- **Zester**

RECIPES

"COOKING IS LIKE LOVE.
IT SHOULD BE ENTERED INTO
WITH ABANDON OR NOT AT ALL."

— HARRIET VAN HORNE

CHAPTER 3

IT'S ALL ABOUT THE BONES

GOLDEN CHICKEN BONE BROTH

YIELD: **3 cups**   PREP TIME: **10 minutes**   COOK TIME: **12 to 24 hours**

I call this a "golden broth" because it sounds warm and comforting, and I decided to go with a nutrient-packed color scheme on this one: yellow onion, turmeric, lemon, and carrot. Yellow and orange vegetables are high in beta-carotene, flavonoids, lycopene, potassium, and vitamin C, which can assist with eye health, fight free radicals, help lower blood pressure and LDL cholesterol, and promote collagen formation, which is a synergistic effect when combined with the yummy collagen from the chicken bones.

Many people let their broth simmer for up to 3 days, but this recipe, made with a little less water than you may be used to, creates a super thick, rich broth after just 24 hours. It's so concentrated that you may be able to dilute it when using it as a flavorful cooking liquid for rice or pasta, but it's perfect warmed up in a mug; the rich, healthy fat has a luxurious mouthfeel, and the lemon and turmeric give you that warming, mouth-tingling feeling. This recipe is perfect for the winter months or when you're feeling a little run-down. **Pro tip:** Pour the broth into an ice cube tray or silicone mold to freeze and store—add a couple of cubes to your morning smoothie or just heat them up when you need a cup.

1 chicken carcass

3 cups filtered water, plus more as needed

2 tablespoons apple cider vinegar

2 large carrots, scrubbed and roughly chopped

1 yellow onion, roughly chopped

2 cloves garlic, roughly chopped

1 lemon, sliced (with peel on)

2 teaspoons fine sea salt

1½ teaspoons ground black pepper

1½ teaspoons turmeric powder

NOTE: *The broth will keep for up to a week in the fridge or up to 3 months in the freezer.*

Put the chicken carcass in a 6-quart slow cooker. Pour in the water and vinegar, making sure the carcass is covered by about an inch of water. Let sit without turning on the heat for 30 minutes. (This is an ideal time to prep the vegetables.)

Add all the vegetables and the lemon slices to the slow cooker and add more filtered water until the ingredients are covered by about an inch of water. Add the salt, pepper, and turmeric powder.

Cook on low for 12 to 24 hours, topping off with more filtered water when the liquid evaporates below the bones.

Remove all the large solids with tongs or a slotted spoon.

Using a fine-mesh strainer, strain the broth into a 1-quart mason jar and discard the solids.

BONE BROTH 101

- To allow plenty of time for the nutrients from both the bones and the vegetables to incorporate into the broth, all bone broths should be cooked for a long time.

- Generally, aim to cook your broth for a minimum of 12 hours and up to 24 hours. The exact cooking time depends on the amount and density of the bones: for example, for a couple of fish carcasses, 12 hours is fine; for a few pounds of buffalo bones, 24 hours is better. When the length of cooking time is given as a range, it's preferable, for maximum nutrition and flavor, to cook the broth for the longer amount of time; that said, the shorter cooking time will still yield a broth rich in both nutrition and flavor.

- I prefer to make bone broth in a slow cooker, but you can cook the broth on the stovetop in a large stockpot over very low heat (barely simmering).

- A properly cooked bone broth, one that's filled with healthy collagen and gelatin extracted from the bones over a long cooking time, will become gelatinous when chilled. Once the broth is heated, it will return to a liquid consistency.

- Larger, sturdier bones can be reused up to three times for broth-making, although the resulting broth will be less nutrient-dense and flavorful each time. When you notice the bones significantly soften or even disintegrate, they're spent and should not be used again.

- Once the broth is chilled, a layer of fat may form across the top. The amount of fat depends on the type of the bones used (beef and lamb bones, for example, have more fat than chicken or fish). You can incorporate this fat layer back into the broth by heating and stirring, or you can simply skim this layer off the top before reheating if you don't want a high-fat broth. It's generally not recommended to use this fat for cooking since it has a high moisture content and won't be easy to work with.

- To reheat broth, gently warm it on the stovetop over medium-low heat for about 5 minutes, or in a mug in the microwave in 30-second increments. Avoid bringing broth to a rolling boil when cooking with it or reheating it to enjoy as a hot beverage, as boiling can break down the proteins in the bones too quickly and essentially boil away much of that rich, fatty goodness—and some cooks say it can impact the flavor, too.

- Have fun with the add-ins and flavor combinations! Use the spices and veggies you like in your broths, and experiment with new ones, too. Consider combinations that optimize health (turmeric and black pepper, for example) as well as add-ins that taste delicious. And, of course, if you have food sensitivities or follow a specific eating protocol, such as low-FODMAP, omit any vegetables or herbs as needed to suit your dietary needs. Make it your own!

- Season the broth to taste (usually with just a pinch of salt) before enjoying it as a hot beverage.

ANTI-INFLAMMATORY TURKEY BONE BROTH

YIELD: **2 quarts**   PREP TIME: **8 minutes**   COOK TIME: **12 to 24 hours**

Erin Skinner is a Registered Dietitian Nutritionist and is board-certified as an Integrative and Functional Nutrition Care Provider. She runs a private practice where she specializes in improving metabolic, digestive, and hormonal health for busy women. Erin actually created a book entirely on broths, so I asked her to contribute a healthy recipe for this book, ideally one that's great for sipping since that's my favorite way to consume broth, and she came through in a big way. Here's what she had to say about this recipe:

"One of the best things about bone broth is that there are infinite ways to customize the flavors. Although I use chicken most often, I will occasionally get some turkey and use those bones for broth. (Hello, post-Thanksgiving—don't throw those bones away!) Aside from a whole turkey, you can also keep your eyes out for turkey legs or thighs as a nice way to mix it up.

"Another way I vary the flavors is with the vegetables, herbs, and spices. This recipe combines the benefits of bone broth with the anti-inflammatory properties of curcumin (found in turmeric) and garlic. Turmeric, garlic, and the amino acids from collagen (from the bones) all have solid evidence showing their anti-inflammatory properties. Your body—and your taste buds—will say thank you!"

1 turkey carcass (from a 12- to 16-pound free-range turkey)

4 quarts filtered water, plus more as needed

¼ cup apple cider vinegar

1 large onion, cut into quarters

6 cloves garlic, smashed with the side of a knife

2 teaspoons turmeric powder

1 bay leaf

2 teaspoons fine sea salt

NOTE: *The broth will keep for up to a week in the fridge or up to 3 months in the freezer.*

Put the turkey bones in a 6-quart slow cooker. Pour in the water and vinegar, making sure the bones are covered by about an inch of water. You may have to break down the carcass slightly to fit it into the slow cooker. Let sit without turning on the heat for 30 minutes. (This is an ideal time to prep the vegetables.)

Add onion, garlic, spices, and salt to the slow cooker.

Cover and cook on low for 12 to 24 hours, checking the water level every 3 hours or so and adding more water as needed to keep the bones covered.

Remove all the large solids with tongs or a slotted spoon.

Using a fine-mesh strainer, strain the broth into two 1-quart mason jars and discard the solids.

BEEF BONE BROTH

YIELD: **3 cups**   PREP TIME: **10 minutes**   COOK TIME: **16 to 24 hours**

Guys, this is about as easy as it gets. Do you have a slow cooker or a large soup pot? Put some bones, vegetables, and water in there, let it cook low and slow for a day, and when you're done, you have a nutrient-dense, delicious broth. There's no secret other than good-quality animal bones and a little patience. You can use this for so many things—cooking rice, flavoring sauces, braising vegetables, as a soup base, in your smoothies—but I enjoy it best warmed up in a mug on a cold, dark winter afternoon, sometimes garnished with sliced green onion.

1 pound beef bones

3 cups filtered water, plus more as needed

3 tablespoons apple cider vinegar

2 large carrots, scrubbed and roughly chopped

1 sweet potato, cubed

1 yellow onion, roughly chopped

3 cloves garlic, smashed with the side of a knife

¼ cup chopped fresh parsley

2 teaspoons fine sea salt

1½ teaspoons ground black pepper

NOTE: *The broth will keep for up to a week in the fridge or up to 3 months in the freezer.*

Put the beef bones in a 6-quart slow cooker. Pour in the water and vinegar, making sure the bones are covered by about an inch of water. Allow to sit without turning on the heat for 30 minutes. (This is an ideal time to prep the vegetables.)

Add the rest of the ingredients, turn the slow cooker to low, and cook for 16 to 24 hours, checking the water level every 3 hours or so and adding more water as needed to keep the bones covered.

Remove all the large solids with tongs or a slotted spoon.

Using a fine-mesh strainer, strain the broth into a 1-quart mason jar and discard the solids.

BONE BROTH FROM THE SEA

YIELD: **3 cups**   PREP TIME: **10 minutes**   COOK TIME: **12 to 15 hours**

Maybe it's my Nova Scotian upbringing and the constant smell of the salty, briny ocean, but I've never been afraid of "fishy" fish dishes. Trout is my favorite fish, and smoked salmon and oysters are up there too. There's something so rich and intense about it—you can't mistake what you're eating. My stepdad used to love to eat dulse, the dried, über-salty seaweed harvested right out of the Atlantic in our backyard, and I developed a taste for those crunchy, deep, bitter veggies too—it's literally like eating the ocean. It turns out that sea vegetables are incredibly healthful, containing high amounts of vitamins, minerals, and specifically iodine. (This makes dulse and other sea vegetables ideal for any of us who have switched from iodine-added table salt to natural sea or rock salt, and may as a result be lacking in iodine.) Iodine can support thyroid function, so it only makes sense to add some sea veggies to your fish broth. Like any broth, you can drink it steaming from a mug during cold months when you need an extra hit of protein, collagen, and vitamins, which is my preferred way to consume it. You can also use it as the cooking liquid for rice served alongside fish, or perhaps even make some fish chowder with it!

1 pound fish carcasses

3 cups filtered water, plus more as needed

2 tablespoons apple cider vinegar

1 white or yellow onion, roughly chopped

3 sheets nori seaweed

5 green onions, roughly chopped

2 cloves garlic, smashed with the side of a knife

1 teaspoon ginger powder

1 teaspoon fine sea salt

NOTE: *Store the broth in glass containers or mason jars; it will keep for up to a week in the fridge or up to 3 months in the freezer.*

Put the fish carcasses in a 6-quart slow cooker. Pour in the water, making sure the bones are covered by about an inch of water. Place the lid on the slow cooker and let the bones sit for 30 minutes without turning on the heat. (This is the ideal time to prep the vegetables.)

Add the rest of the ingredients, turn the slow cooker to low, and cook for 12 to 15 hours; at 12 hours, the bones will be soft and mostly translucent, and the vitamins and minerals will have leached into the broth. For a more concentrated flavor, keep it going for up to 15 hours. Every few hours, check the broth and top off with filtered water when it evaporates below the bones.

Remove all the large solids with tongs or a slotted spoon.

Using a fine-mesh strainer, strain the broth into a 1-quart mason jar and discard the solids.

SAVORY OATMEAL BREAKFAST BOWL

YIELD: **2 servings**   PREP TIME: **5 minutes, plus time to refrigerate overnight**   COOK TIME: **10 minutes**

If I had to describe my eating style accurately but concisely, I'd probably say I'm "meat-based Paleo plus oatmeal." I love oatmeal. Some people are absolutely against grains, and some don't tolerate oats, but quick-cooking gluten-free oats have been one of the carb mainstays in my life since my bodybuilding days, and they still hold a special place in my heart and my belly. They're just so warming, comforting, and satisfying. As a slow-burning complex carbohydrate, oats keep me full way longer than toast, pastries, or even a protein-heavy breakfast can. I've always been the weirdo frying eggs and mixing them into my oats, usually with a little cinnamon. That particular combination may not go mainstream, but oats are a versatile carbohydrate that is easy to prepare and works really well in sweet or savory dishes, for breakfast or any other time. Incorporating bone broth adds another layer of depth and complexity as well as nutrition; if you use a mild chicken broth, you can still make sweeter oatmeal (think about adding cacao powder, coconut milk, and berries) without tasting the broth, and using a more intense broth works well in the savory option here. I love recipes that are easy, are not too precious, and don't require super specific amounts or instructions. With this one, all you really need is bone broth, oats, and some creativity.

1 cup gluten-free quick-cooking steel-cut oats

1 cup chicken bone broth, plus more as needed (page 52)

1 tablespoon unsalted grass-fed butter or bacon fat

2 large eggs

Fine sea salt and ground black pepper and/or other spices such as garlic powder or paprika (optional)

2 green onions, thinly sliced

¼ cup shredded cheese of choice

NOTE: You can store the broth-soaked oats in an airtight jar in the fridge for up to 3 days, but I don't recommend storing this one longer than a day or so after it's prepared; the oats are bound to get mushy.

Put the oats and bone broth in a pint-sized mason jar; seal, place in the refrigerator, and allow the oats to absorb the broth overnight.

Just before serving, cook the eggs: Melt the butter in a cast-iron skillet over medium heat and cook the eggs over-easy or to your liking.

While the eggs are cooking, heat the oats in the microwave for about 50 seconds or in a small pot on the stovetop over medium-low heat for about 3 minutes, until warmed through and softened but not mushy. (You want them to retain an al dente chew.) You can add more broth as needed depending on your preferred consistency; I like mine a little thicker, so less broth is needed.

Divide the oats between 2 small soup bowls, then top each bowl with an egg. Season with salt and black pepper (or other spices) to taste, if desired.

Evenly sprinkle the green onions on top and, finally, add the shredded cheese, allowing it to melt. (If you have a small kitchen blowtorch, you can use it to melt/crisp up the cheese.) Serve hot.

MAPLE SWEET POTATO BONE BROTH SMOOTHIE BOWL

YIELD: **2 servings**   PREP TIME: **10 minutes, plus 30 minutes to chill (not including time to cook sweet potato)**

This is essentially a comforting bowl of Thanksgiving goodness, especially if you top it with pecans. This recipe makes a thick smoothie that you eat with a spoon from a bowl; add some pretty toppings and make yourself #instafamous. If you like it extra thick and chilly, freeze the bone broth in ice cube trays and blend those into the mix; you can also add more milk or water and pour it into a glass for a drinkable breakfast treat if you prefer. And of course, you can switch any or all of this out—replace the sweet potato with banana, add cacao powder or flavored collagen powder, or throw in some berries or whatever is seasonal and delicious to you. I recommend using a milder-flavored bone broth, like chicken, without added savory spices or other flavors— that way, you won't even taste the broth. It is essentially there for invisible nutrition hidden in a tasty dessert bowl. Miracles can happen!

1 cup chicken bone broth (page 52), chilled

1 cup full-fat coconut milk or other milk of choice, chilled

1 medium sweet potato, cooked, cooled, and peeled

1 (½-inch) piece fresh ginger, finely chopped

1 teaspoon ground cinnamon

1 teaspoon turmeric powder

½ teaspoon ground cardamom

2 teaspoons maple syrup

1 teaspoon vanilla extract, or seeds scraped from 1 vanilla bean

1 scoop unflavored grass-fed collagen powder

1 teaspoon cacao powder (optional)

FOR TOPPING (OPTIONAL):

Toasted pecans, unsweetened shredded coconut, dark chocolate chips, coconut sugar, or other topping of choice

Put all the ingredients except the optional toppings in a blender and blend until smooth, about 2 minutes.

Put the blender jar in the fridge for at least 30 minutes to chill the smoothie, then pour into 2 bowls. If desired, sprinkle with your favorite toppings before serving.

SUPER SEXY BONE MARROW

YIELD: **4 servings**   PREP TIME: **2 minutes**   COOK TIME: **20 minutes**

This recipe is almost too silly to write (buy an orange; peel the orange; eat the orange), but I'm including it because people may see marrow on a restaurant menu or on Instagram and think that it's a treat for "hard-core" or advanced meat-eaters, when it's not. Bones are inexpensive and can be found at any butcher shop; it's easier and faster than roasting a chicken or sweet potato; and it's one of the most decadent, sexy things you can eat. It's rich, warm, salty, buttery, and chock-full of health-promoting collagen and micronutrients that our bodies need. It tastes delicious spread like butter across some warm, crispy toast, but the most satisfying way to enjoy it is straight up, on its own. There is something especially primal about this recipe, perhaps more than others in this book, because it's so visually arresting, and the taste is so melt-in-your-mouth sumptuous. If bone marrow isn't a known aphrodisiac, it should be. I highly recommend you roast some for your next home-cooked date meal, and feel free to let things get messy. You're welcome. (Bonus points if you gnaw on the bones when you're done or save them to use in my beef broth recipe on page 58.)

4 cross-cut beef femur (a.k.a. marrow) bones, about 2 inches long

Coarse sea salt

Preheat the oven to 450°F.

Place the bones cut side up on a rimmed baking sheet lined with parchment paper. Sprinkle the bones with coarse salt.

Cook until the marrow is softened and starts to bubble and brown, about 20 minutes. To test the softness of the marrow, stick a fork or toothpick into it; the marrow should be gelatinous and soft all the way through.

WHIPPED BONE MARROW BUTTER

YIELD: **about ½ cup**   PREP TIME: **2 minutes**   COOK TIME: **25 minutes, plus 15 minutes to refrigerate**

This condiment is so rich and delicious, I can't believe how easy it is to make. And it's a serious upgrade to generic unsalted butter (which, granted, is pretty good, but this is way more impressive!). It has a rich, tongue-coating umami taste that makes everything you eat it with seem infinitely more decadent. It goes well with anything—spread on a slice of warm crusty bread, slathered onto vegetables prior to roasting, or melted on top of a baked potato, dolloped on a grilled steak, the list goes on! Hot tip: Save the marrow bones to use in my beef broth recipe on page 58.

2 beef femur (a.k.a. marrow) bones (about 1½ pounds), canoed (cut lengthwise)

1 tablespoon finely chopped fresh parsley

1 tablespoon finely chopped fresh thyme

Fine sea salt and ground black pepper

NOTE: Bone marrow butter will keep in the fridge for many weeks, just like dairy butter, although after it's refrigerated it will lose its whipped consistency and harden, also like butter. All you have to do is leave it out until it reaches room temperature; you can then use it as is or blend it again in a blender or food processor if you prefer the whipped consistency.

Preheat the oven to 425°F. Line a rimmed baking sheet with foil or parchment paper.

Place the marrow bones marrow side up in the prepared pan and roast until the marrow is bubbling and soft when you stick a fork in it, about 25 minutes.

Remove from the oven and let cool; when the bones are cool enough to handle, scoop the marrow into a small bowl with a spoon and place the bowl in the refrigerator to cool completely, about 15 minutes. When the marrow has cooled, it will have the consistency of softened butter.

Put in a blender or food processor with the herbs and season to taste with salt and pepper. Blend on medium speed until white and fluffy.

PORK HOCK HODGEPODGE

YIELD: **6 servings**   PREP TIME: **20 minutes**   COOK TIME: **2 hours 15 minutes**

Hodgepodge is the somewhat adorable maritime name for a stew made with heavy cream, flour, green beans (or whatever veggies are around), and pork hock. Although pork hock doesn't fit neatly into most definitions of offal, I wanted to include this recipe to highlight the tastiness and versatility of bone-in cuts like this that may be overlooked in favor of "easier" or more common pieces. In my interpretation of this humble Nova Scotian dish, I swapped out the cream, flour, and beans for ingredients that I prefer, but this version has the same spirit: it's about incorporating what's handy and in season into something comforting and nourishing. I've never been much of a soup person, and I famously tell anyone who asks (which isn't many people, since soup isn't an exciting conversation piece) that if I can't chew it, it's not a meal. Well, you can definitely sink your teeth into this, with its thick, creamy consistency and big hunks of sumptuous pork. I used to think that a delicious stew would be a lot of work and using bone-in meat added more effort, but this recipe is surprisingly easy—it's perfect for a lazy winter Sunday when you're home in your PJs hanging out in the kitchen anyway.

½ cup diced yellow onions

5 carrots, peeled and chopped

¼ cup extra-virgin olive oil, plus more for drizzling if desired

Smoked sea salt and ground black pepper

1 large sweet potato, peeled and chopped into 1-inch pieces

4 cups chicken or beef bone broth (page 52 or 58)

1 fresh pork hock (about 1 pound)

1 teaspoon paprika

1 large bunch kale, destemmed and chopped or torn into bite-sized pieces

In a 6- or 8-quart pot over medium heat, cook the onions and carrots in the olive oil with a pinch each of salt and pepper until tender, about 10 minutes.

Add the sweet potato and stir until combined.

Add the bone broth and pork hock. Cover, reduce the heat to medium-low, and simmer until the potatoes are soft and the hock is cooked through, about 2 hours.

Remove the pork hock from the pot and place on a cutting board to cool, then remove the pot from the heat and let cool until no longer piping hot but still warm, about 20 minutes.

Transfer the contents of the pot to a food processor or blender, add the paprika, and process until smooth. Add salt and pepper to taste, then return the mixture to the pot.

Chop the pork into ½-inch pieces. (I included the skin, but you don't have to.) Transfer the chopped pork to the pot and return it to medium-low heat.

Add the torn kale to the pot and stir until fully mixed and the kale is warmed but not yet wilted.

Ladle into serving bowls, top with a little salt and/or olive oil, and enjoy.

NOTE: *This soon-to-be-famous Pork Hock Hodgepodge will keep for up to a week in the fridge or up to a month in the freezer. I used smoked salt in this recipe since so many similar recipes call for smoked ham hock; finishing with the smoked salt is an especially nice touch. You can also add a nice smoky flavor with smoked paprika.*

" **THERE IS NO LOVE**
SINCERER THAN THE
LOVE OF FOOD. "

-GEORGE BERNARD SHAW

CHAPTER 4

FROM THE NECK UP

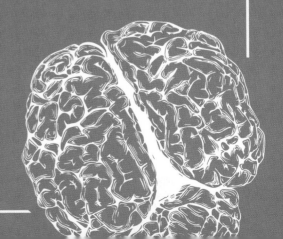

TONGUE IN TOMATO SAFFRON SAUCE

YIELD: **6 to 8 servings**   PREP TIME: **30 minutes**   COOK TIME: **3 hours**

Diana Jarrar-Solomon is the founder of MAGICdATES, a snack company that makes better-for-you date-based treats without added sugar. I am a huge fan of Diana and her company, and the sincerity and enthusiasm she has for healthy eating is infectious. Although we've spent only a little time together in a professional capacity, we bonded online over our love of off-cuts, and I asked her if she would contribute a recipe based on what she loves to eat with her family. Here's what Diana said about this recipe:

"Few things bring back the memory of home for me like the date fruit or a lamb's head perched on top of rice. Growing up in Damascus, Syria, every meal was a small celebration. Not a bite or an animal part wasted. Our food system in the US is undergoing an evolution, and we're questioning whether our food choices are making us sick. I'm going back to basics and embracing the traditions with which I was raised: lots of plants and some meat, raised humanely, eaten entirely. This recipe is full of Persian flavors like saffron, inspired by my love for my husband and his family. Like my mom, I use a typical Syrian method of boiling meat with aromatics that fill the air with a smell that sings, 'Welcome home.' I hope your home is filled with nostalgic aromas that your kids will one day yearn for and will connect them to their past."

1 quart filtered water

1 beef tongue (about 2 pounds), rinsed

1 tablespoon black peppercorns

1 tablespoon cardamom pods

2 large or 3 small bay leaves

Fine sea salt and ground black pepper

2 tablespoons unsalted grass-fed butter, divided

1 yellow onion, sliced

1 bell pepper, any color, sliced

½ cup white wine

1 (28-ounce) can whole peeled tomatoes

Juice of 2 lemons

2 cloves garlic, finely chopped

2 tablespoons date syrup (see Notes, page 76)

2 teaspoons ground Omani lemons (optional; see Notes, page 76)

½ teaspoon saffron threads, preferably Persian (see Notes, page 76)

¼ cup chopped fresh parsley, for garnish

Pour the water into a 6-quart stew pot set over medium heat. When the water is warm, add the tongue, peppercorns, cardamom pods, and bay leaves. (Do not add the salt yet. Tongue is a tough and strong muscle, and the meat won't tenderize completely if cooked in salted water.) Cover and simmer gently over medium-low heat for about 2 hours 15 minutes; do not allow the water to boil. Every 20 to 30 minutes or so, skim off any foam or impurities that come to the top, as the cooking broth will be used later. During the

NOTES: *Persian saffron is the highest quality you can get; you can find it online or at Persian or Middle Eastern markets. It has a deep red color throughout; it doesn't have orange or yellow ends.*

Omani lemons are actually dried limes; they're a staple in Persian cuisine and easily found at Persian markets or online. You can grind them yourself in a spice grinder or buy it preground. Omani lemons add a complex and tangy flavor that can't be duplicated.

I used date syrup in this recipe, but you can use a sweetener of your choice (honey or maple syrup for example); you can find date syrup online on Amazon, at many large groceries like Whole Foods, and at Mediterranean markets.

This dish will keep in the fridge for about 3 days but is best when eaten fresh.

last 30 minutes of cooking, add 2 tablespoons of salt. The tongue is done when you pierce it with a fork and it slides through easily.

Turn off the heat. Carefully remove the tongue from the broth and allow it to cool, about 15 minutes. Set the broth aside.

When the tongue is cool enough to handle but still warm, remove the skin by first cutting a slit in at the base of the tongue (the wider end) and then pulling the skin away with your fingers. It will peel off easily. Slice the tongue crosswise in ¼-inch-thick medallions and lightly salt both sides.

Heat a large, deep sauté pan over medium heat and add 1 tablespoon of the butter. Sear the tongue slices for about 1 minute on each side; do this in batches, if needed, to avoid crowding the pan. Remove the tongue from the pan and set aside.

Add the remaining tablespoon of butter to the pan and sauté the onion slices until they begin to caramelize, 5 to 7 minutes. Add the bell pepper and sauté for 2 to 3 minutes, until the pepper is softened.

Pour in the wine and deglaze the pan.

Puree the whole peeled tomatoes in a blender or food processor, then add the puree to the pan along with the lemon juice, garlic, date syrup, Omani lemon (if using), saffron, a pinch each of salt and pepper, and ⅓ cup of the reserved tongue broth. Allow the sauce to simmer for 20 minutes. You may add more or less broth depending on the sauce consistency you prefer. Save the rest of the broth for making soups and stews.

Add the tongue slices back to the pot and allow to simmer in the sauce for 10 minutes.

Serve in shallow bowls and garnish with lots of fresh parsley.

SLICED BEEF TONGUE SANDWICHES

YIELD: **8 servings**   PREP TIME: **25 minutes**   COOK TIME: **6 hours 12 minutes**

Essentially, what you're doing here is creating a high-fat, juicy, tender cold cut for sandwiches (or cold cut plate, or just a snack you can eat on its own). Sliced tongue has been a popular option in Jewish delis forever, so I'm not creating anything new here. If you cook tongue properly, it will be incredibly juicy with a nice chew, and it goes great with a fresh crusty bread like sourdough, some mayo and stone-ground mustard, lettuce, and tomato slices and/or pickled vegetables.

1 beef tongue (about 2 pounds), rinsed

3 tablespoons unsalted grass-fed butter

Coarse sea salt and ground black pepper

Sandwich fixings of choice

NOTE: *Tongue can be used in almost all the ways you might use beef tenderloin—as sandwich meat, as here in this recipe, as a warm main dinner course, or chopped and added to a cold salad for lunch. Leftovers are great repurposed for hash, too (see page 80). The cooked tongue will keep in the fridge for up to a week.*

Put the tongue in a 6-quart slow cooker or soup pot and add just enough water to cover the tongue. Cook the tongue on high if using a slow cooker, or over medium heat if using a soup pot, until it is tender and can be easily punctured with a fork, 4 to 6 hours. Remove the tongue to a cutting board and let cool to the touch, about 15 minutes.

Using a sharp knife, make a slit through the skin at the base of the tongue (the wider end) and peel away the skin; it should be easy to remove. Cut the tongue crosswise into ½-inch-thick slices and pat dry with a paper towel.

Heat the butter in a 12-inch cast-iron skillet over medium heat. Sear the slices in batches until browned and crispy around the edges, about 3 minutes on each side. Season with salt and pepper to taste.

Use the seared meat slices to make sandwiches, using the fixings of your choice.

TONGUE HASH WITH PEPPERS, ONIONS, AND POTATOES

YIELD: **2 servings**   PREP TIME: **10 minutes**   COOK TIME: **15 minutes**

The inclusion of eggs in this dish lends itself to breakfast, but this is an anytime meal that's filling and full of protein and flavor. This is a great way to use up leftover tongue you may have from another recipe; as you may have noticed, a beef or buffalo tongue is pretty big—2 pounds or more of meat!

2 tablespoons ghee or unsalted grass-fed butter

½ red onion, diced

½ red or yellow bell pepper (or a combination), diced

Coarse sea salt

½ pound small new potatoes, halved and baked (leave peels on)

6 ounces leftover cooked beef tongue, chopped (see page 78)

4 large eggs

1 Hass avocado, diced, for garnish

Ground black pepper

NOTE: *This hash will keep in the fridge for up to 3 days but is best when eaten fresh out of the skillet.*

Heat a 12-inch cast-iron skillet over medium-high heat. Melt the ghee in the pan, then add the onion and bell pepper and season with a pinch of salt. Cook, stirring occasionally, until the onion is soft and translucent, about 4 minutes.

Add the potato and cook, stirring occasionally, until warmed through, about 4 minutes.

Add the tongue and cook, stirring occasionally, until warmed through, about 4 minutes.

Using a spoon or spatula, create 4 wells in the hash and carefully crack an egg into each well.

Lower the heat to medium and cook until the eggs have reached your desired doneness. Transfer the hash to 2 serving plates, garnish with the avocado, season with salt and pepper to taste, and serve.

GREENFIELD FAMILY TONGUE TACOS

YIELD: **12 soft tacos, plus leftover tongue**   PREP TIME: **20 minutes**   COOK TIME: **8 hours 10 minutes**

Ben Greenfield is a human performance consultant and *New York Times* bestselling author of thirteen books, including *Beyond Training* and *Boundless*. He's a hugely influential podcaster, trainer, and biohacker, a frequent contributor to health and wellness publications and websites, and a highly sought-after speaker—and he also happens to be a fan of organ meats. I've interviewed Ben a number of times, and I love his family-centric approach to health; he includes his twin boys, River and Terran, in cooking, fishing and hunting, mindfulness, exercise, and so much more, and his kids have developed a passion for healthy eating as well. They even have their own podcast talking about the food they make! I was so excited when the boys submitted this recipe for tongue tacos because with it they demonstrate that healthy eating can be simple and fun, organ meats need not be intimidating, and teaching children the value of nutritious, nose-to-tail eating can be a fun and valuable family activity.

TONGUE:

1 large white onion, cut into wedges

10 cloves garlic, smashed with the side of a knife

1 beef tongue (about 2 pounds), rinsed

2 teaspoons dried oregano leaves

2 tablespoons ghee or unsalted grass-fed butter, for the pan

Fine sea salt and ground black pepper

PICKLED RADISHES AND ONIONS:

2 bunches radishes, thinly sliced

1 white onion, thinly sliced

¾ cup apple cider vinegar

3 tablespoons honey, preferably raw

4 teaspoons fine sea salt

1 teaspoon red pepper flakes

FOR SERVING:

12 (6-inch) tortillas

6 cups shredded lettuce

6 ounces Cotija cheese or cheese of choice, crumbled or shredded

3 Hass avocados, sliced

3 limes, cut into wedges

Put the onion wedges, garlic, tongue, and oregano in a 6-quart slow cooker and cover with boiling water. Set the slow cooker to low and cook until the tongue is tender and easily pierced with a fork, 6 to 8 hours.

Remove the tongue from the slow cooker and let cool for about 15 minutes, until cool enough to handle.

Meanwhile, make the pickled radishes and onions: Put all the ingredients in a medium bowl and mix well. Let sit on the counter for at least 1 hour before serving.

NOTE: *Both the tongue and the pickled radishes and onions will keep in the fridge for up to a week.*

When the tongue is cool to the touch, use a sharp knife to make a slice across the base of the tongue (the wider end), then peel off the thick outer layer of skin. Cut the tongue into ½-inch dice.

Heat the ghee in a large skillet over medium-high heat. Add the tongue and season with salt and pepper. Sauté until browned and nicely seared.

To assemble the tacos, divide the diced tongue among the tortillas and top with the pickled radishes and onions, shredded lettuce, cheese, and avocado. Serve with lime wedges and enjoy!

SLOW-COOKED SWEET BEEF CHEEKS WITH CARDAMOM AND VANILLA

YIELD: **4 servings**   PREP TIME: **5 minutes**   COOK TIME: **6 hours**

Despite the recipe's name, don't worry about this dish tasting candy-sweet; it won't. The warming, sweet-spicy flavors of the cardamom, cinnamon, and vanilla serve to balance the rich fattiness of this cut of meat. Cheeks are—you guessed it—the cheek meat of, usually, a cow (although you can sometimes find pork cheeks and fish cheeks, which are tasty treats too!). They are often incorrectly seen as a tough cut, despite being fatty, because when braised and cooked low and slow, the result is a tender, soft, deeply flavorful piece of meat that can pull apart like brisket. Beef cheeks can be found at most butcher shops and specialty meat shops, and are high in protein, healthy fat, and amino acids (just like regular beef muscle meat). This dish actually tastes better the day after you make it, when it's had more time to sit in its own juices. Pair it with crispy pan-fried polenta rounds, like I did, or with rice, cauliflower rice, or zucchini noodles—ideally something with a little texture that will absorb all the amazing juices.

2 pounds beef cheeks

1 teaspoon coarse sea salt

½ teaspoon ground cardamom

½ teaspoon ground cinnamon

½ teaspoon garlic powder

½ teaspoon onion powder

½ teaspoon paprika

Seeds scraped from 1 vanilla bean

FOR SERVING:

Pan-fried polenta rounds (see Notes) or other side of choice

Lime wedges

Using a sharp paring knife, trim any excess fat from the beef cheeks, then rinse them with cold water and pat dry with a paper towel.

Combine the salt, spices, and vanilla seeds in a small bowl. Rub the spice mixture all over the meat.

Put the beef cheeks in a 6-quart slow cooker, cover, and cook on low for 6 hours (no need to add water). When done, the meat will be tender, almost like brisket.

Divide the meat among 4 plates or shallow bowls. Serve with the polenta rounds, the rich broth from the slow cooker, and lime wedges.

NOTES: The pan-fried polenta rounds shown in the photo are easy to make; I buy precooked polenta packed in a tube, so that all I need to do is slice it and pan-fry it with some butter until it's crispy on the outside.

This dish will keep in the fridge for up to a week.

PROVENÇAL BEEF CHEEK DAUBE

YIELD: **6 servings**   PREP TIME: **5 minutes, plus 24 hours to marinate**   COOK TIME: **3 to 4 hours**

Tania Teschke is a writer and photographer who is passionate about French food and wine, nose-to-tail eating, and regenerative agriculture. She is the author of the award-winning book *The Bordeaux Kitchen: An Immersion into French Food and Wine, Inspired by Ancestral Traditions*. Tania has learned from cooks, butchers, chefs, farmers, and winemakers in France and holds a diploma in wine science and tasting from the University of Bordeaux. We met through my work with *Paleo Magazine,* and I absolutely love her cookbook: she illustrates beautifully how to blend French tradition with ancestral tradition, showing that decadent, beautiful food can be healthy, honoring our bodies' needs and desires. This is Tania's story about this recipe:

"Recipes in France are handed down from master to apprentice, grandparents to children and grandchildren, cook to cook. L'Abbé Brison, a priest and theologian in Provence, passed this stew recipe on to my good friend Tony Mellili, a trained hotelier and chef from the Savoie region of France. I met Tony and his partner, Dominique, in Paris in 2003, renting a studio apartment from them for several months while working there. I ate more often in their adjoining apartment than in mine, and they introduced me to French home cooking long before I was interested in it. They are credited with launching me on a lifetime exploration of cheese, wine, and good French living. Having moved to Provence several years ago, Tony has learned the recipes of Provence, and he passed this one on to me.

"A daube is a saucy stew, simmered over low heat for several hours, often marinated first in wine. What makes it Provençal are the olives, tomatoes, and shrubby herbs of thyme, rosemary, and bay leaf, indigenous to Provence, that make up the bouquet garni.

"Beef cheeks (the jowl of the animal) belong to the French categorization of les abats, what we call organ meats. In France, they are traditionally a cheaper cut of meat, and this type of stew is typically served in winter."

MARINADE:

2½ pounds beef cheeks

6 cloves

1 red onion, halved

1 carrot, cut into 3 or 4 large pieces and then halved lengthwise

1 orange quarter (with peel)

Bouquet garni (3 bay leaves and 1 [3-inch] sprig each of thyme and rosemary)

Pinch of mixed peppercorns

1 (750-ml) bottle red wine

STEW:

¼ cup extra-virgin olive oil

1 red onion, chopped

3½ ounces bacon, chopped

¼ cup cassava flour

2 medium tomatoes, peeled and crushed

3 carrots, peeled and chopped into 3 or 4 large pieces and then halved lengthwise

1 clove garlic, halved

1 teaspoon coarse sea salt

½ cup filtered water

¼ cup black olives (with pits)

Chopped fresh parsley or grated Parmesan cheese, for garnish (optional)

NOTES: *For the best flavor, you can marinate the beef cheeks for 24 hours. Order your beef cheeks from the butcher and have them trim the excess fat, as cheek can be chewy!*

For the wine, use a full-bodied, tannic red with an alcohol content of 13% to 15%, such as the wines of southern France.

This recipe calls for black olives, but green olives will work as well. Keeping the pits in the olives during cooking adds to the flavor of the stew.

Leftovers will keep in the fridge for up to 3 days.

Using a sharp paring knife, trim any excess fat from the beef cheeks, then rinse them with cold water and pat dry with a paper towel. Cut into 1½- to 2-inch cubes.

Insert the cloves into the red onion half, then put the clove-studded onion in a large bowl along with the cubed beef cheeks, carrot, orange quarter, bouquet garni, and peppercorns. Pour the wine over the ingredients. Cover the bowl and place in the refrigerator to marinate for at least 6 hours or up to 24 hours.

Remove the meat from the marinade and set it aside in a large bowl. Remove the bay leaves and thyme and rosemary sprigs and set them aside in another bowl. Reserve the marinade and peppercorns for cooking. Discard the marinated carrot, onion, and orange quarter, as these would make the stew taste bitter.

Heat the olive oil in a large stainless-steel or cast-iron stew pot over high heat. (*Note:* For this recipe, enameled cast-iron is preferable: it's ideal for long cooking dishes with acidic ingredients like red wine.) Fry the onion for about 5 minutes, until transparent. Add the beef cheeks all at once and cook, stirring frequently, for 3 to 5 minutes, until browned. Add the bacon and continue cooking and stirring occasionally for 3 minutes. Sprinkle in the flour and stir until mixed. If the mixture becomes a bit dry, remove from the heat so as not to burn the ingredients.

Stir in the tomatoes and place the pot back over the heat. Stir in the fresh carrots, garlic, reserved herbs from the marinade, reserved marinade liquid, and salt. Bring to a boil, then lower the heat to a simmer. Simmer for 3 to 4 hours, until the ingredients are softened and the broth has reduced and thickened.

Midway through the cooking time, stir in the water. Add the olives during the last hour of cooking. Season to taste with salt. Garnish with fresh parsley or grated Parmesan, if desired. Serve immediately or let cool and reheat the following day.

SCRAMBLED BRAINS AND EGGS

YIELD: **4 servings**   PREP TIME: **20 minutes, plus 1 hour to soak**   COOK TIME: **20 minutes**

I could get into so many "my brain is scrambled" jokes here, but let me just be up-front about this recipe: I get it, brain is a tough sell. It looks exactly like what it is, and that in itself seems extreme, because most of us in the Western world aren't used to seeing it as an ingredient. You probably remember scary news stories (from decades ago) of mad cow disease—which, if I'm being specific, isn't from eating brain, but from eating infected beef that has been exposed to tissue from a sick cow's brain and spinal cord. Today, diseases like mad cow are very rare. So here's a practical rebuttal to that fear of the unknown: first, if you're getting fresh offal from a trusted source—ideally harvested locally—there's no more increased risk of contamination or bacteria than there would be from eating any other part of the animal. And if you can get past the squeamish aspect of eating such a recognizable organ (which I believe you can, or you wouldn't have bought this book), you'll discover that brain is straight-up delicious. Usually sourced from veal (but sometimes also beef and lamb), brain is mild and creamy, not gamey or strong-tasting at all—in fact, it has a similar texture to delicious scrambled eggs, which is why this recipe exists. (I'm far from the first person to come up with this combo.) Since veal is the most common and most mild-flavored brain, that's what I recommend for this recipe.

Brain is full of healthy fats, and if you can find it, it's a special and nutritious treat. Fair warning—if you live in North America, brain isn't going to be easy to come by. I live in a big city, and I visited a number of local butchers and Asian markets inquiring about brain; I even called the local farm where I source all my other off-cut meats, and every person I spoke to looked at me like I was asking for *human* brain. I finally came across an old-school butcher shop committed to offering a nose-to-tail experience, and I was able to indulge in an incredibly unique and delicious breakfast. Again, these recipes are all about honoring the animal, experimenting with unique flavors and textures, and sometimes putting in a little extra work for a sizable reward.

1 veal brain

Filtered water

½ teaspoon coarse sea salt

1 green onion, or a small handful of fresh chives

8 large eggs

2 tablespoons heavy cream

2 tablespoons unsalted grass-fed butter

Wash the brain, remove all the membranes, and cut away the white brain stem at the base. Soak the brain in a bowl of cold filtered water with the coarse sea salt for 1 hour.

Remove the brain from the water, place in a medium pot, and cover with fresh filtered water. Bring to a boil and cook for 10 minutes; the brain will go from milky white to grayish and become more firm and solid, yielding more resistance when poked with a fork.

While the brain is cooking, slice the green onion (or chives).

Avocado slices (optional)

Fine sea salt and ground black pepper

NOTES: *Just to be extra careful, I wouldn't store this dish—if you're going to all the trouble to make brains and eggs, you might as well dig in and eat them, right? Not to mention that even eggs, when cooked and then refrigerated, tend to get rubbery and not so tasty.*

As with most of these recipes, you should feel free to spice things up (literally, with your favorite spices) and add cheese or whatever else you enjoy on eggs. I like mine with a dash or two of hot sauce!

Remove the brain from the cooking water and place in a colander to drain, then put it in an ice bath until it is cool enough to handle, about 5 minutes.

Remove the cooled brain from the water, pat dry with a paper towel, and use a sharp knife to cut it into ¼-inch dice.

Crack the eggs into a medium bowl, then add the cream and whisk until smooth.

Heat the butter in a 12-inch cast-iron skillet over medium heat. Pour the eggs into the skillet, then add the diced brain. Using a silicone spatula, cook, continually stirring so it doesn't stick, until the eggs are set.

Remove from the heat and plate. Top with the sliced green onion and avocado slices, if desired, and season with fine sea salt and pepper to taste.

SLOW-ROASTED LAMB NECK WITH RICE

YIELD: **4 servings**   PREP TIME: **30 minutes, plus time to marinate overnight**   COOK TIME: **6 hours**

Whether it's the neck or any other cut, lamb has the most delicious, meaty, savory flavor; it's one of my favorite protein sources! When lamb neck is marinated and slow-cooked, the meat is rich and fork-tender and falls off the bone. Often, when a recipe calls for neck, it's chicken or turkey neck (usually thrown into a pot to make broth or browned in a skillet, respectively) or lamb or goat neck (both generally braised or slow-roasted). You can find delicious nose-to-tail dishes featuring goat and lamb in Caribbean, Moroccan, and Middle Eastern dishes, among many other cuisines. The neck meat of these larger animals doesn't taste any different than the rest of the muscle meat, and it's cost-effective since it's not a high-demand cut.

This particular dish was inspired by one of my most memorable meals, at a tiny spot called Duck's Eatery in New York City's East Village. It was typical New York: crowded, dark, loud, but unpretentious considering the quality of the food the restaurant served. The dish I ordered was goat's neck over rice, and it was served bone-in. It stuck with me because it was so flavorful and tender but so simple. I went with lamb here because I wanted to do something a little different—and lamb is a little easier to find where I live—but both are delicious options!

2 lemons, seeded and diced (leave peels on)

Cloves from 1 head garlic, minced

1 cup extra-virgin olive oil

1 tablespoon coarse sea salt, plus more for garnish

1 tablespoon ground black pepper

1 teaspoon ground cumin

2 lamb necks (about 1 pound)

2 cups white rice, cooked in lamb or beef bone broth (page 58)

¼ cup chopped fresh parsley leaves, for garnish

To make the marinade, put the lemons, garlic, olive oil, salt, pepper, and cumin in a small bowl and mix to combine.

Put the necks in a small casserole dish, pour the marinade over top and massage into the necks with your hands, then cover and refrigerate overnight.

When ready to cook the necks, preheat the oven to 200°F. Remove the necks from the marinade and place them on a rack set inside a rimmed baking sheet. Discard the marinade. Roast the necks until the meat is very tender, about 6 hours.

Remove the pan from the oven and let the necks cool a bit; when cool enough to handle, cut the meat from bone and plate atop the rice. Garnish with the parsley, a squeeze of lemon, and salt, and serve.

NOTES: *When rice (or cauliflower rice, if you're avoiding grains) is cooked in a rich bone broth, it elevates any dish it's served with. This dish is perfect for impressing guests at a dinner party or for a holiday meal if you're tired of turkey or ham.*

Leftover cooked neck and rice will keep in the fridge for up to 5 days.

"TELL ME WHAT YOU **EAT**, AND I WILL TELL YOU WHAT YOU ARE."

-JEAN ANTHELME BRILLAT-SAVARIN

CHAPTER 5

EAT YOUR HEART OUT

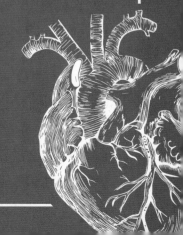

PORK HEART SAUSAGE SHEET PAN DINNER

YIELD: 6 servings, plus leftover sausages   **PREP TIME:** 1 hour, plus 1 hour to soak casings and time to dry sausages overnight   **COOK TIME:** 25 minutes

I don't expect everyone to go out and buy meat grinders with sausage making attachments, but I do want to illustrate this process as one that is totally doable even for a novice chef, like me. There's a little finessing required to fill the natural casings: pork intestine is very strong but surprisingly delicate at the same time, and overfilling or twisting the casing will result in burst sausages. With that said, learning to make sausages from scratch gave me a deep appreciation for butchers and others making these delicious treats for us—they're more work than we give them credit for! It's also really fun to mix your own ingredients, and figure out what flavor and spice profile you enjoy. My butcher recommends a 4:1 ratio of fatty muscle meat to organ meat, although you can play with this ratio depending on your taste.

SAUSAGE:

2 pounds ground pork (70% lean; preferably ground pork shoulder)

6 ounces pork heart or pork liver, cleaned (see page 98 or 120) and cubed, or a mixture of both

2 cloves garlic, minced

1 green onion, finely chopped

½ cup fresh oregano leaves, finely chopped

1½ teaspoons ground cumin

1 teaspoon paprika

½ teaspoon cayenne pepper

1 teaspoon fine sea salt

1 package natural hog casing packed in salt (1.3 inches in diameter and about 78 inches long)

2 pounds creamer potatoes

5 apples, such as McIntosh

1 tablespoon extra-virgin olive oil

½ teaspoon fine sea salt

¼ teaspoon ground black pepper

⅛ teaspoon ground cumin

SPECIAL EQUIPMENT:

Meat grinder with sausage attachment

Put the ground pork and organ meat through a meat grinder together. For a smooth consistency, run the meat through the grinder twice.

Put the ground meat mixture in a large bowl and add the garlic, green onion, oregano, spices, and salt. Using your hands, mix the meat and seasonings together until evenly combined. (To taste test, cook a small patty in a skillet, taste, and add more salt or spices as desired.) Place the meat in the fridge to chill while you work on the next step.

Rinse the sausage casing thoroughly with water, then soak in a bowl of filtered water for 1 hour, until it is rehydrated and soft.

Thread the entire sausage casing over the sausage filling attachment on the meat grinder, leaving about 5 inches hanging off the end; do not tie off the end.

Feed the meat into the hopper for the sausage filling attachment while using your other hand to guide the sausage coming out of the attachment; the casing will automatically come off of the attachment with the movement of the meat through the tube. Let the sausage come out in one long coil, leaving about 5 inches of empty casing on either end.

About every 5 inches down the coil (depending on how long you want your sausages) pinch the sausage and spin around three times—clockwise the first time, counterclockwise the second, and so on, so they stay coiled. Make a small knot in the casing at either end, cutting off any extra casing. If you notice any air bubbles in the casing, prick lightly with a pin to remove the air so the sausages don't burst during cooking.

Let the sausages dry on a wire rack in the fridge overnight. The next morning, cut the links apart with scissors.

Preheat the oven to 350°F. Place 6 of the sausages on a rimmed baking sheet lined with parchment paper. (If you're making these all at once, you will need more than one pan.)

Clean, dry, and roughly chop the potatoes and apples into 1-inch pieces.

In a medium bowl, toss the apples and potatoes with the olive oil, salt, pepper, and cumin. Place in a single layer around the sausages on the baking sheet.

Bake for about 25 minutes, until the potatoes begin to brown, the apple skins start to soften and "wrinkle," and the sausages begin to brown.

Remove from the heat, plate, and serve!

NOTES: *If you don't have a meat grinder or sausage-making equipment and don't plan on buying any, you can ask your butcher to mix some ground organ meat into your ground beef or pork, season the mixture as you like, and make sausage patties yourself at home.*

Feel free to experiment with the veggies for the sheet pan dinner as well: Brussels sprouts, carrots, and cauliflower would all work great here; I've just always liked the textural and sweet/starchy contrast of apples and potatoes, and I think this combination makes for a delicious and hearty cooler-weather meal.

You can generally find natural sausage casing at butcher shops; unused casing can be stored in an airtight container in the fridge, submerged in salt water, for months.

The cooked sausages will keep for up to a week in the fridge or up to 2 months in the freezer.

How to Clean Heart

For all hearts except chicken hearts: Trim the hard, white exterior fat and any visible membranes with a sharp paring knife, and cut out visible arteries, veins, or other non-muscle meat from the top of the heart, then rinse thoroughly with cold water. You should end up with a piece of relatively smooth, blood-red muscle meat. *(Any further cutting or prep would be individual to the recipe.)*

Note that most larger animal hearts will be sourced from a local farm and butcher, and you'll notice they have already been cut or sliced open for quality control (to ensure the organ is healthy and safe and didn't contain any bugs or parasites).

For chicken hearts: Chicken hearts can be purchased at many grocery stores. They tend to be already cleaned and removed of any excess material and are generally ready to cook after being rinsed thoroughly in cold water. (**Pro tip:** Squeeze the hearts while rinsing to ensure you get rid of trace amounts of blood inside them.)

DEER DIP SANDWICHES

YIELD: **4 servings**   PREP TIME: **10 minutes**   COOK TIME: **35 minutes**

No matter how many times I try to tell people that heart is just a muscle like any other part of the animal we're used to eating, sometimes people need to experience it in a completely familiar, comforting dish to be convinced. So why not put it in a sandwich? I've made heart sandwiches a few times in an attempt to encourage friends to eat something they find a little scary in a non-scary way. For this recipe I thought I'd up the offal factor by adding the French dip aspect—dipping your already delicious sandwich into some hot, savory bone broth. It completely alters the texture and the way you eat your sandwich, changing it from an easy handheld lunch favorite into something warmer, messier, and much more fun.

Cooked medium and thinly sliced, you can think of this as a new take on roast beef, and if you want to skip the dip, sliced deer heart tastes just as good with sauerkraut and Dijon mustard as roast beef does. Perfectly cooked and seasoned sliced heart has the ideal texture to hold up to a hearty sandwich.

1 deer heart (about 2 pounds), cleaned (see page 98)

Fine sea salt and ground black pepper

4 soft gluten-free Kaiser or bread rolls

2 tablespoons unsalted grass-fed butter

1 cup beef bone broth (page 58)

Stone-ground mustard, to taste

4 slices provolone cheese (optional)

NOTES: *If deer hearts are hard to come by, you can swap in beef, elk, lamb, or whatever is available.*

Once cooked, the meat will keep in the fridge for up to 10 days—all you have to do is throw it in a skillet to heat it up before serving or, in true cold-cut style, eat it straight from the fridge with a dollop of mustard and a sprinkle of salt!

Preheat the oven to 350°F. Place a wire rack on a rimmed baking sheet.

Season the outside of the heart with salt and pepper.

Put the heart on the rack, then place the pan in the oven and bake until browned on the outside and firm all the way through but still pink on the inside, about 30 minutes. Remove from the oven and let sit for 10 minutes.

Slice the heart as thinly as possible (think sliced roast beef).

Cut the rolls down the middle, butter both sides, and place the halves cut side down in a large skillet over medium heat until just starting to crisp, about 4 minutes.

Bring the bone broth just to a simmer in a small saucepan over medium heat, about 5 minutes, or in the microwave for about 1 minute.

Spread the toasted buns with mustard, then layer the sliced heart on the bottom bun, add a slice of provolone cheese, if desired, and top with the top half of the bun. Carefully dip your sandwich into the hot broth (just a dip; you don't want the bread disintegrating) and dig in! You may need a fork and knife.

HEARTY NIGHTSHADE-FREE CHILI

YIELD: **6 servings**   PREP TIME: **25 minutes**   COOK TIME: **1 hour 35 minutes**

My friend Cristina Curp is a certified Nutritional Therapy Practitioner and former restaurant chef with a degree in anthropology. Her love of food, and particularly the use of real food to heal, inspired her popular food blog and wellness site, *The Castaway Kitchen*. A "food as medicine" advocate, she is author of the *Made Whole* and *Made Whole Made Simple* cookbooks and cohost of *Body Wise Podcast*. Her Cuban roots inform a lot of her food, as do her own struggles with autoimmune conditions; she took to the kitchen to find solutions to an inflammatory skin condition as well as postpartum challenges and has found incredible relief and benefit in a personalized, nutritious, whole-foods diet. I asked for her to create a comfort food dish incorporating organ meat for this book, and this recipe is the delicious result. Made with bone broth, finely chopped mushrooms, lots of alliums, and a little sweet potato, this long-simmering chili is aromatic, flavorful, and truly hearty!

3 tablespoons extra-virgin olive oil

1 large white onion, diced

4 cloves garlic, minced

Leaves from 2 sprigs fresh rosemary, finely chopped, plus more leaves for garnish if desired

1 bay leaf

3 teaspoons fine sea salt, divided

2 cups chopped cremini mushrooms

1 pound beef heart, cleaned (see page 98) and ground (see Notes)

1 pound 85% lean ground beef

12 ounces bacon, coarsely ground

2 teaspoons garlic powder

2 teaspoons ground black pepper

2 teaspoons ground cumin

2 teaspoons dried oregano leaves

½ teaspoon ground white pepper

¼ teaspoon five-spice powder

1 large sweet potato, peeled and diced

5 cups beef bone broth (page 58)

Heat a 6-quart Dutch oven or other heavy-bottomed pot over medium heat. When it's hot, pour in the olive oil. Add the onion, garlic, rosemary, bay leaf, and 1 teaspoon of the salt. Sauté until the onion is tender and aromatic, about 10 minutes.

Add the mushrooms and cook, stirring often, until very tender and browned. Then mix in the heart, beef, and bacon. Use a whisk to break up the meat, stirring often until it's very crumbly and begins to brown, about 10 minutes.

Stir in the remaining 2 teaspoons of salt and all the seasonings. Keep mixing until the meat mixture is cooked through and finely crumbled (no big chunks of beef).

Stir in the sweet potato and bone broth. Bring to a simmer over medium heat and simmer for 10 minutes, then reduce the heat to low and cover the pot. Cook, stirring every 20 minutes, for 1 hour. Garnish with extra rosemary, if desired. Serve hot!

NOTES: *To grind the heart, cut it into 1-inch chunks and run them through a meat grinder. I use the Kitchen Aid stand mixer attachment for this task. Alternatively, you can ask your butcher to grind the heart for you before you take it home.*

Beef heart is a really meaty but very lean organ, so adding some bacon to the mix balances out the protein-to-fat ratio. The chili will keep for up to a week in the fridge or up to a month in the freezer.

COLD-HEARTED SALAD

YIELD: **2 servings**   PREP TIME: **5 minutes**   COOK TIME: **10 minutes**

You may be thinking, this salad is so easy, I didn't even need a recipe! And I'm thinking, you may be right, but when was the last time you made a chicken heart salad? I rest my case. It's easy, it's delicious, and it's just as simple as a chicken breast salad, except this one is more fun, flavorful, and nutrient dense. As with all of my favorite recipes, you have a lot of flexibility to customize this one and really make it your own favorite salad. Switch up the greens (arugula and kale are great choices), use strawberries or blackberries instead of apples, use whatever dressing or cheese or nuts you want. This is just a combination I really like, and the hearts are really—sorry, upcoming pun—the heart of the recipe; everything after that is a fun bonus. The hearts add a little pop of tender, chewy, meaty goodness and a unique textural contrast but mild taste that doesn't overwhelm whatever salad you're making.

Avocado oil spray, or
1 tablespoon ghee

**8 ounces chicken hearts,
cleaned (see page 98)**

4 cups mixed salad greens

**2 medium-crisp or crisp apples,
such as McIntosh, sliced**

**1 ounce shaved Parmesan or
pecorino cheese**

½ cup raw pecans

**3 tablespoons The Easiest Salad
Dressing Ever (page 224)**

NOTE: *The cooked chicken
hearts will keep in the fridge for
up to a week; store the salad
components separately and
dress only what you plan to eat
right away, or the salad will get
soggy quickly!*

If using a barbecue grill, lightly oil the grill grates with avocado oil spray; if using a skillet, oil it with the ghee. Preheat the grill to medium heat or heat a 12-inch cast-iron skillet over medium heat.

Pat the hearts dry and grill or pan-fry them until cooked through (they'll be browned and firm, but not rubbery) and starting to get a bit of a sear, about 7 minutes. Remove from the pan and set aside to cool while you prep the salad.

Divide the salad greens between 2 plates, then evenly top the greens with the apple slices, Parmesan cheese, pecans, and chicken hearts. Drizzle with the dressing and enjoy!

SAUCY, SPICY LAMB HEARTS

YIELD: **4 servings** PREP TIME: **5 minutes** COOK TIME: **20 minutes**

Lamb hearts are, predictably, a little bigger than chicken hearts but smaller than beef hearts, so they're kind of a happy medium: they have a rich lamby flavor but are still quick and easy to cook like smaller hearts are. This recipe shows off the ease and versatility of this cut of meat. You don't have to roast it for hours or hide it in something elaborate: just pan-fry it with some butter and spices, and you have a delicious protein source to throw on top of a salad or starchy side dish.

2 lamb hearts, cleaned (see page 98)

¼ cup blanched almond flour

2 teaspoons coarse sea salt

1 teaspoon smoked paprika

½ teaspoon cayenne pepper

¼ cup (½ stick) unsalted grass-fed butter

½ small yellow onion, diced

⅓ cup chicken or beef bone broth (page 52 or 58)

FOR SERVING:

4 cups arugula

1 lemon wedge

Coarse sea salt and ground black pepper

NOTE: *These saucy lamb hearts will keep in the fridge for up to a week.*

Pat the hearts dry and cut them into 1-inch cubes.

Mix together the flour, salt, paprika, and cayenne pepper in a medium bowl. Dredge the heart pieces in the flour mixture.

Heat the butter in a 12-inch cast-iron skillet over medium-high heat. When it's hot, place the heart pieces in the pan and pan-fry for 4 minutes per side, until cooked through. (You can cut a piece to ensure that it's firm and cooked on the inside.) Turn the pieces over carefully with tongs so you don't break off the crust.

Add the diced onion to the pan and allow to soften for about 4 minutes, scraping up any browned bits on the bottom of the pan with a wooden spoon. Add the bone broth and turn the heart pieces until they're coated. Let the sauce reduce for 3 to 4 minutes, until it has a gravylike consistency.

Plate the saucy hearts on top of a bed of arugula and top with a squeeze of lemon juice and some salt and pepper, if desired.

PALEO PHO

YIELD: **4 servings**   PREP TIME: **15 minutes**   COOK TIME: **45 minutes to 1 hour, depending on charring method**

I'm honored that Diane "V" Capaldi offered up this recipe for my book. Also known as the Paleo Boss Lady (you can see why we get along!), V is a TEDx speaker, chef, recipe developer, and award-winning advocate to raise awareness for those in need and those requiring support to get healthier. She has created a brand and a movement around conscious living and supporting, encouraging, and lifting people up, and she's truly one of the most positive and inspiring people I know. She brought me to tears when I interviewed her for the *Paleo Magazine* Radio podcast—the only guest to do so! Here is V's story about this recipe:

"I moved to Venice Beach, California, close to fifteen years ago to help heal my body from multiple sclerosis (MS). Weather plays a key role in my well-being, and Venice fit the bill for aiding my healing journey. The first year I lived in Venice, people were inviting me out for pho, and the Italian girl in me had no idea what they were talking about. Pho is a huge dish in LA, so I decided to try my hand at making a version that includes heart to make it even more nutrient-dense. Needless to say, I love this dish all year long and no longer have a fear of pho! Each bite supports our mitochondria, and that, for me, is always a huge win."

2 white onions, quartered

2 (2-inch) pieces fresh ginger, cut in half lengthwise

2 cinnamon sticks

2 black peppercorns

2 whole star anise

2 cloves

2 teaspoons ground coriander

2 quarts bone broth, any type (see Notes)

2 teaspoons fish sauce

2 cups roughly chopped carrots (peels on)

2 pounds beef heart, cleaned (see page 98)

2 zucchini

2 green onions

2 limes

2 tablespoons chopped fresh basil, for garnish

2 tablespoons chopped fresh mint, for garnish

Char the onions and ginger: Hold the onion quarters and ginger pieces directly over a flame with tongs until charred, which takes just a few minutes. If you don't have a gas stovetop or you prefer a more hands-off technique, you can char them in the oven. To use the oven method, preheat the oven to 400°F and line a rimmed baking sheet with parchment paper. Put the onions and ginger pieces on the lined baking sheet and bake until slightly charred, about 20 minutes.

In a large saucepan over medium-low heat, dry toast the cinnamon sticks, peppercorns, star anise, and cloves until fragrant, about 5 minutes. Be careful not to burn them; turn at least once. Add the ground coriander and toast for another 2 minutes.

NOTES: *Feel free to use premade bone broth or incorporate one of the homemade bone broths from this book. (I recommend the beef broth on page 58.)*

Pho is best eaten fresh due to the delicacy of the ingredients, but it will keep in the fridge for up to 3 days (store the broth separately from the meat).

Add the bone broth, fish sauce, carrots, and charred onions and ginger to the toasted spices. Bring to a boil, then reduce the heat, cover, and simmer for 30 minutes.

Place the heart in the freezer for about 10 minutes; this makes it easier to slice.

Meanwhile, spiral-slice the zucchini into noodles, chop the green onions, and quarter the limes; set aside.

Remove the heart from the freezer, place on a cutting board, and cut into the thinnest slices possible; they will cook in the hot broth.

Remove the broth from the heat, strain through a colander, and set aside.

Divide the zucchini noodles among 4 serving bowls and top each with a few thin slices of heart and some sliced green onions. Ladle the hot broth into the bowls, completely covering the meat, and allow the meat to cook for about 5 minutes. (It will be cooked to medium at this point.)

Serve, allowing each person to add their own fresh basil, mint, and lime garnishes.

ALMOND BUTTER, RASPBERRY, AND HEART PEMMICAN

YIELD: **12 servings**   PREP TIME: **10 minutes, plus 1 hour to refrigerate**   COOK TIME: **10 hours**

Traditionally, pemmican was made by North American Native peoples, who mixed whatever meat was handy with animal fat and sometimes berries; the meat was often smoked or dried, and the resulting product was hearty, nutrient and calorie dense, and long-lasting. This version is a little updated, somewhere between pemmican and a homemade protein bar. Yes, there is meat in it, but replacing the animal fat with almond butter and honey balances the flavors surprisingly well. With the raspberries, the end result has a definite peanut-butter-and-jelly vibe, with a little salty, umami taste on the end from the dried meat.

½ cup chicken hearts, cleaned (see page 98)

½ cup ground chicken

1 cup raspberries

½ cup raw shelled sunflower seeds

¼ cup smooth almond butter (unsalted and unsweetened), plus more if needed

2 teaspoons honey, preferably raw

2 tablespoons unflavored grass-fed collagen powder

1 teaspoon fine sea salt

2 teaspoons coconut oil, for the pan

NOTE: *Switch out the berries, seeds, and meat for the ingredients of your choosing; the seeds can be replaced by nuts and the almond butter by another nut or seed butter or any animal fat you have on hand. Just keep the ratios the same! This pemmican will keep for up to 3 weeks in the fridge or up to 3 months in the freezer.*

Preheat the oven to 200°F. Line 2 rimmed baking sheets with parchment paper.

Pat the hearts dry and pulse in a food processor or high-powered blender until finely chopped but not liquefied.

Spread the ground chicken and chopped chicken hearts in a thin, even layer on one of the lined baking sheets, spreading it all the way to the edges of the pan. Roll it out with a rolling pin if necessary.

Spread out the berries and sunflower seeds on the other lined baking sheet.

Place both pans in the oven and allow to dry slowly for 10 hours. All the ingredients should be completely dry and crispy, with no moisture remaining. (Crack open the oven door for a few minutes every couple of hours to let any moisture escape.)

Remove from the oven and let cool. Put the berries, seeds, and dried meat in a food processor or high-powered blender and mix until ground into a meal consistency, with no clumps or chunks. Transfer the mixture to a medium bowl.

In a small microwave-safe bowl, warm the almond butter and honey in the microwave for 30 seconds, or until softened, then add to the bowl with the meat mixture.

Combine the ingredients, including the collagen and salt, with wet hands; the mixture will have a slightly grainy texture but should stick together. If needed, add more almond butter a tablespoon at a time until it does stick together.

Grease a glass container, about 5 by 7 inches, or an 8½ by 4½-inch loaf pan, with the coconut oil and place the mixture inside, pressing it down firmly with your hands.

Refrigerate for at least 1 hour before cutting into portions and serving.

GRILLED CHICKEN HEART SKEWERS

YIELD: **6 servings**   PREP TIME: **15 minutes, plus time to marinate overnight**   COOK TIME: **10 minutes**

This recipe is so simple, so delicious, and so crowd-pleasing. It's also an friendly entry into the world of heart, since chicken hearts are mild and meaty and easy to work with. They are an excellent addition to a summer BBQ, a great protein-filled appetizer, or a quick Paleo-friendly entrée next to a mixed salad or cauliflower rice. I eat chicken hearts about once a week, and I'm not tired of them yet!

MARINADE:

⅓ cup extra-virgin olive oil

3 tablespoons red wine vinegar

½ teaspoon fine sea salt

½ teaspoon ground cumin

¼ teaspoon ground black pepper

¼ teaspoon cayenne pepper

1 pound chicken hearts, cleaned (see page 98)

1 red onion, chopped into 1-inch pieces

1 bell pepper, any color (or a combination), chopped into 1-inch pieces

Lime wedges, for serving

SPECIAL EQUIPMENT:

6 (10-inch) wood skewers, soaked in water for 1 hour

NOTE: *Leftover skewers will keep for up to 5 days in the fridge.*

Put all the ingredients for the marinade in a medium mixing bowl and mix well. Pat the hearts dry and add them to the marinade, tossing them to coat. Cover the bowl and place in the fridge to marinate overnight.

Preheat a barbecue grill to high heat, or preheat a grill pan on the stovetop over high heat.

Skewer the hearts with a slice of onion or bell pepper between them, for a total of 4 or 5 hearts per skewer. Grill until slightly charred on the surface and medium-rare inside, about 4 minutes per side, turning the skewers over midway through cooking. Serve immediately with a squeeze of lime.

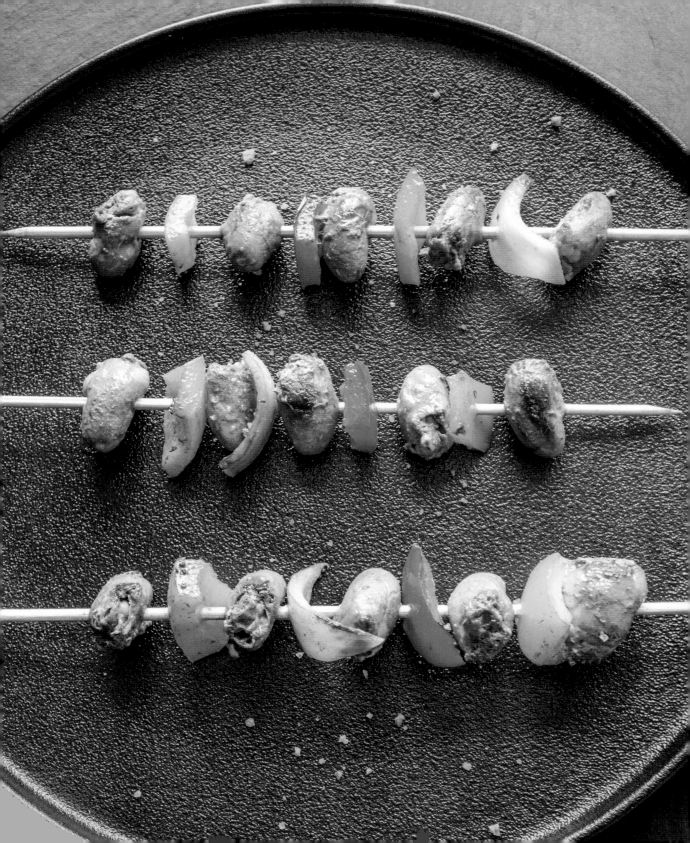

BEEF HEART JERKY

YIELD: **12 servings**   PREP TIME: **10 minutes, plus time to marinate overnight**   COOK TIME: **10 hours**

Maybe I shouldn't be confiding in you about this, but I was so surprised at how tasty this recipe turned out! I actually enjoyed my homemade beef heart jerky more than the high-end stuff you can buy at the grocery store. The marinade has the perfect blend of umami, salty, and just a little bit sweet, and the richness of the heart makes for a really flavorful and satisfying taste that isn't too gamey but is much more interesting than typical beef jerky. It's a great snack for outdoorsy types or folks who want their protein on the go, and it's an easy way to prepare leftover meat that you don't want to go bad.

2 pounds beef heart, cleaned (see page 98)

¼ cup coconut aminos

2 tablespoons maple syrup

¼ cup apple cider vinegar

Juice of ¼ lemon

½ teaspoon ground black pepper

½ teaspoon garlic powder

½ teaspoon onion powder

½ teaspoon coarse sea salt

1 tablespoon sesame seeds, for garnish (optional)

SPECIAL EQUIPMENT (recommended):

Food dehydrator

With a sharp knife, slice the heart into ¼-inch-thick strips (think beef jerky!). Put the strips in a glass bowl.

To make the marinade, mix together the rest of the ingredients except the sesame seeds. Taste and add more spices or other ingredients to your liking (depending on whether you want the end result to be more spicy, salty, sweet, or tangy).

Once you achieve the flavor you like, pour the marinade over the heart in the bowl and mix well with your hands to ensure that all the strips are covered. Cover the bowl and place in the fridge to marinate overnight.

In the morning, take out the meat strips and pat them dry with a paper towel. At this point, you can sprinkle them with the sesame seeds if you like. Place the strips in a dehydrator, leaving space between them. Set the dehydrator to 160°F for 10 hours. Remove the jerky from the dehydrator when it is fully dried and has the consistency of beef jerky.

NOTES: *I've always wanted an excuse to buy a dehydrator, and this was it—but if you don't have one, you can turn your oven to its lowest setting (200°F for most ovens), lay the strips on a wire rack set on a rimmed baking sheet, and bake for about 10 hours. You'll want to check it every few hours and also crack the oven door every couple of hours to let the moisture being released from the meat escape.*

Store the jerky in an airtight glass container in the fridge; if it's nice and dry, it should be fine for up to a month.

STUFFED BUFFALO HEART

YIELD: **8 servings**　PREP TIME: **10 minutes**　COOK TIME: **1 hour**

This may be the recipe I'm most proud of—it looks and tastes beautiful and sophisticated, but it's ultimately just simple, real, nourishing food. Hearts from bigger animals, such as buffalo, do have a stronger, slightly gamey taste, but they're rich in iron and protein. Here, the stronger flavor is balanced out perfectly by the sweeter bacon-rich filling. This gorgeous dish is an example that if I—an inexperienced wannabe chef—can create something so beautiful, I'm confident you can as well.

8 ounces bacon, chopped

1 yellow onion, chopped

8 ounces button mushrooms, chopped (about 2 cups)

1 buffalo heart (about 3 pounds), cleaned (see page 98)

SPECIAL EQUIPMENT:

Butcher's twine

NOTE: *If you can't find buffalo heart, you can use bison or beef heart in this recipe. A buffalo heart is, excuse the pun, a hearty meal indeed—we were eating this for leftovers for a week, which is about how long you'd want to keep it, stored in the fridge. The best way to reheat it is to throw it back on a cast-iron skillet over medium-high heat with some ghee for 5 to 7 minutes.*

Preheat the oven to 350°F. Place a wire rack on a rimmed baking sheet.

In a 12-inch cast-iron skillet over medium heat, fry the bacon and onion until the bacon is browned and crisp and the onion is browned, about 8 minutes. Using a slotted spoon, remove the bacon and onion from the pan and set aside on a plate lined with a paper towel, leaving the bacon fat in the pan.

Add the mushrooms to the skillet and cook until softened, about 5 minutes. Transfer the mushrooms to the plate with the bacon and onion and allow to cool. Leave any remaining bacon fat in the pan; you will use it to sear the heart. When the bacon mixture is cool, pat it with a paper towel to soak up any excess grease.

Pat the heart dry, then slice it in half horizontally, like you're cutting a hamburger bun.

Cut about 2 feet of butcher's twine and lay it across a plate; place 1 half of the heart on top of the twine, cut side up. Spoon the bacon, onion, and mushroom filling on top of the heart, then place the second half of the heart over the filling. Wrap the twine around the heart several times, both lengthwise and widthwise, tightly enough that the 2 pieces of heart come together and the filling isn't spilling out, and tie off. Cut off any excess twine.

Set the cast-iron skillet with the reserved bacon fat over high heat. (If more fat is needed, add a tablespoon of butter or ghee.) When the fat is hot, carefully place the heart in the pan and fry for about 3 minutes on each side just to brown the exterior—be careful that you don't lose the filling while turning it over!

Transfer the heart to the wire rack on the baking sheet and place the pan in the oven. Bake for 40 minutes for medium-rare (as pictured) or up to 10 minutes more for medium-done meat. (If you cook heart beyond medium, it can become rubbery.)

Let the heart sit for about 10 minutes before removing the twine and cutting into ½-inch-thick slices.

" PEOPLE WHO
LOVE TO EAT
ARE ALWAYS
THE BEST PEOPLE. "

-JULIA CHILD

CHAPTER 6

LIVER IS THE WURST

PROSCIUTTO-WRAPPED CHICKEN LIVERS

YIELD: **6 servings (as an appetizer)**   PREP TIME: **15 minutes, plus 1 hour to soak livers**   COOK TIME: **10 minutes**

Wrap anything in prosciutto and it'll be a crowd-pleaser! Here, the rich, creamy sweetness of chicken livers pairs really well with crispy, salty prosciutto. (You can use thin-sliced bacon, too.) You definitely want to eat this delicious and protein-packed appetizer immediately, as soon as the livers come out of the skillet.

6 whole chicken livers, split into 2 lobes each (12 pieces total), cleaned (see sidebar)

Ground black pepper

12 slices prosciutto

Fresh thyme or rosemary sprigs, for garnish

SPECIAL EQUIPMENT:

2 (9-inch) wood skewers, soaked in water for 1 hour

Pat the livers dry with a paper towel. Lightly season with pepper.

Using 1 strip of prosciutto per lobe, wrap the strips tightly around the liver pieces so that they are entirely covered.

Using the skewers to hold the prosciutto in place, insert the prosciutto-wrapped livers onto the skewers, 6 per skewer.

Preheat a barbecue grill to medium heat, or preheat a grill pan on the stovetop over medium heat.

Grill the skewers, turning them every few minutes, until the prosciutto is crispy and the livers are just cooked through, about 7 minutes. Serve hot with a garnish of fresh thyme or rosemary.

NOTE: *If you have leftovers, store them in the fridge for up to 5 days; to reheat, throw them back in a skillet over medium heat with some butter until recrisped, about 3 minutes.*

How to Clean Livers

To clean all animal livers, first rinse them in cold water, then trim any white connective tissue or membranes with a sharp paring knife and soak them for 1 hour in cold water with 1 tablespoon of apple cider vinegar or a pinch of salt. Proceed with the recipe as written.

VENETIAN LIVER AND ONIONS

YIELD: **2 servings**   PREP TIME: **5 minutes, plus 1 hour to soak liver**   COOK TIME: **35 minutes**

My favorite meal in Ottawa, Ontario, Canada (and I promise I'm not just saying this for the book) is the Venetian liver and onions from North and Navy, a northern Italian-inspired restaurant in Centertown. It's a beautiful spot with excellent food (the meatballs aren't too shabby, either) and a favorite spot for a girls' dinner. One night I approached the head chef, Adam Vettorel, about contributing the recipe to my book. He kindly obliged, and here's what he had to say about this shockingly delicious dish:

"Liver and onions is a prized dish all over the Veneto region of Italy, and a sign of wealth. Historically, liver was among the most prized cuts from pork and calves, and as such they commanded a high price. Venice, being the economic center of a vast empire, became associated with this rich delicacy. In this recipe, sweet onions add a nice counterpoint to the strong-tasting organ—this dish is perfect for converting someone who is otherwise squeamish around offal."

14 ounces calf liver, cleaned (see page 120) and cut into ½-inch-wide strips

Fine sea salt

2 tablespoons grapeseed or avocado oil (see Notes)

3 tablespoons unsalted grass-fed butter

2 medium sweet onions, such as Vidalia, cut into thin strips

3 ounces small button mushrooms, cleaned

2½ cups red wine

Ground black pepper, for finishing

Preheat a 12-inch cast-iron skillet over high heat.

Pat the liver pieces dry and season generously with salt. Add the oil to the hot pan, then sear the pieces as quickly as possible, a few minutes on each side.

Transfer the liver to a paper towel–lined plate to soak up the excess oil and stop it from cooking any further. It should still be pink in the middle.

Remove the skillet from the heat and let cool for a minute, then carefully pour off the remaining oil.

Return the skillet to the stovetop over low heat and add the butter, onions, and mushrooms. Cook low and slow for at least 20 minutes, stirring often, until the onions are translucent and soft.

Add the wine and increase the heat to medium. Simmer until the wine is reduced by half.

Return the liver to the pan for a few minutes, just to warm it up again. Portion onto plates with the pan gravy, sprinkle with pepper, and enjoy!

NOTES: *According to Chef Vettorel, the most common mistake made with liver is overcooking it; overcooked liver tastes like metal. A little pink on the inside is okay! You can substitute pork liver if you can't source calf's liver. He uses grapeseed or avocado oil in this recipe because of the high smoke point; butter and olive oil have lower smoke points and aren't ideal for quick, hot cooking.*

This dish is excellent served with polenta or mashed potatoes to soak up all the rich gravy, and it is best when eaten fresh.

CRISPY FRIED CHICKEN LIVERS

YIELD: **8 servings (as an appetizer)**   PREP TIME: **5 minutes, plus 1 hour to soak livers**   COOK TIME: **25 minutes**

These fried livers pair perfectly with my avocado aioli and make a tasty starter for any meal or game-day snack buffet. Crunchy and salty on the outside, slightly creamy and rich on the inside, and full of vitamins, minerals, and protein—it definitely beats your typical deep-fried appetizer.

1 pound chicken livers, cleaned (see page 120)

1 large egg

1 cup blanched almond flour

½ cup gluten-free oat flour

2 teaspoons fine sea salt

1 teaspoon smoked paprika

½ teaspoon ground black pepper

¼ teaspoon cayenne pepper

¼ teaspoon garlic powder

3 tablespoons ghee, divided

½ cup Avocado Aioli (page 218) or your dipping sauce of choice, for serving

NOTE: *These livers will keep for up to a few days in the fridge, but we all know that anything breaded and fried is going to taste best when eaten right away. If reheating, simply throw the livers in a cast-iron skillet over medium heat with a bit of cooking fat for about 5 minutes.*

Pat the livers dry with paper towels and set aside in a glass bowl.

Beat the egg in a small bowl, then pour it over the livers until they are fully covered.

Combine the flours, salt, and spices in another small bowl or shallow dish.

Preheat a 12-inch cast-iron skillet over medium-high heat. Once hot, add 1 tablespoon of the ghee. (You'll be frying the livers in 3 batches, and you want to make sure there's a generous amount of fat in the pan at all times, so add another tablespoon of ghee each time you add a new batch to the pan.)

Using your hands, dredge one-third of the egg-coated livers in the flour mixture until well coated. Gently place in the skillet so they're not touching.

Cook, undisturbed, for 4 to 5 minutes. Using tongs, gently flip and cook for an additional 3 to 4 minutes on the other side. Try to move the livers as little as possible so you don't break apart the crust. Remove carefully and set aside on a wire rack to cool.

Repeat with the remaining ghee, livers, and breading.

Serve warm with the aioli.

CHICKEN LIVER MOUSSE

YIELD: **12 servings**   PREP TIME: **10 minutes, plus 1 hour to soak livers and 2 hours to chill**
COOK TIME: **5 minutes**

I have high hopes that this will be a crowd-pleasing addition to your appetizer spread or charcuterie board—it's rich, lightly sweet, and just boozy enough to be a hit. It's easy to make and so packed with protein and vitamins that I literally feel healthier after I've had a few servings of this stuff. You can switch out the heavy cream for coconut milk and the tequila for apple cider vinegar if you're keeping it strict Paleo, but having tried both versions, I think the original recipe tastes much better! My Sea Salt Paleo Crackers (page 210) make a great scooper for this spread, as do apple slices, raw veggies, or slices of crusty bread.

8 ounces chicken livers, cleaned (see page 120)

½ cup (1 stick) unsalted grass-fed butter, melted, plus 2 tablespoons for cooking

1 small shallot, finely diced

¼ cup heavy cream or full-fat coconut milk

¼ cup white tequila or apple cider vinegar

1 teaspoon fine sea salt

1 teaspoon fresh thyme leaves

½ teaspoon ground black pepper

½ teaspoon ground cinnamon

½ teaspoon ground nutmeg

Pat the livers dry.

Melt 2 tablespoons of the butter in a 12-inch cast-iron skillet over medium heat.

Add the shallot and cook until it begins to soften, about 3 minutes, then add the livers and sauté for about 3 minutes per side. The insides of the livers will still be a little pink.

Transfer the shallot and livers to a blender. Add the ½ cup of melted butter, the cream, tequila, salt, thyme, pepper, cinnamon, and nutmeg. Blend on high speed until completely smooth, about 2 minutes.

Pour the mousse into a pint-sized mason jar and place in the refrigerator to chill for at least 2 hours, until it is fully cool and has a texture similar to soft-serve ice cream.

NOTE: This mousse will keep for up to a week in an airtight container in the fridge. The top layer may change color slightly, which is fine—remove it if you want to. You can also freeze the mousse for up to 2 months; just defrost it in the fridge for a day before serving.

CHOPPED LIVER

YIELD: **12 servings**   PREP TIME: **10 minutes, plus 1 hour to soak livers and 1 hour to chill**   COOK TIME: **15 minutes**

This spread is similar to the Chicken Liver Mousse on page 126, but with no alcohol and a chunkier texture. The inclusion of schmaltz and mustard make it a little more savory than the rich-sweet mousse, but both recipes are great ways to turn nutrient-dense liver into a spread that is great on a charcuterie board or dolloped on vegetable crudités, Sea Salt Paleo Crackers (page 210), or Paleo Beauty Bread (page 206).

3 tablespoons schmaltz or duck fat, divided

1 large white onion, roughly chopped

1 pound chicken livers, cleaned (see page 120)

Fine sea salt and ground black pepper

2 large eggs, hard-boiled, peeled, and chopped

2 tablespoons stone-ground mustard

½ teaspoon paprika

Raw vegetables, crackers, or bread, for serving

NOTE: *This spread will keep for up to 10 days in the fridge or up to a month in the freezer.*

Put 1 tablespoon of the schmaltz in a 12-inch cast-iron skillet over medium heat. Add the onion and sauté until soft and starting to brown, about 4 minutes. Transfer the cooked onion and fat from the pan to a food processor or blender.

Pat the livers dry, then add the remaining 2 tablespoons of schmaltz to the skillet and fry the livers in a single layer, working in batches if needed, until browned on the outside and still slightly pink on the inside, 3 to 5 minutes per side; season with salt and pepper while cooking.

Add the cooked livers, hard-boiled eggs, mustard, and paprika to the food processor or blender and pulse, scraping down the sides as needed, until roughly chopped and combined, about 30 seconds. You want all the ingredients to be mixed without creating a completely smooth paste; it should have a bit of texture.

Cover and place in the fridge to chill until completely cool, at least 1 hour, before serving.

DUCK LIVER TERRINE WITH BLUEBERRY SAUCE

YIELD: **12 servings**   PREP TIME: **10 minutes, plus 1 hour to soak livers and time to refrigerate terrine overnight**
COOK TIME: **2 hours 30 minutes**

This combination is so decadent and yet so healthy. The terrine retains a little bit of texture from the figs and shredded duck, and its denser consistency makes it easy to cut into perfect slices for a charcuterie board. The richness of the liver is perfectly complemented by the warm sweetness of the blueberry sauce—which is also a welcome addition to sweeter dishes like ice cream, scones, or pancakes. You can, of course, switch out the duck liver and leg for chicken if you wish, but I think this version has a deeper, richer flavor.

1 pound duck livers, cleaned (see page 120)

Fine sea salt

½ cup chicken bone broth (page 52)

1½ teaspoons unflavored grass-fed gelatin

8 ounces bacon, divided

2 green onions, thinly sliced

2 cloves garlic, minced

1 tablespoon unsalted grass-fed butter

2 cups cooked and shredded duck leg

½ cup fresh figs, finely chopped

1 teaspoon dried thyme

½ teaspoon ground cloves

BLUEBERRY SAUCE:

2 cups blueberries (fresh or frozen)

½ cup maple syrup

1½ teaspoons vanilla extract

Pinch of fine sea salt

To make the terrine:

Preheat the oven to 350°F.

Pat the livers dry and sprinkle with salt; set aside.

Put the bone broth in a small bowl, add the gelatin, and allow to bloom, about 5 minutes.

Heat a 12-inch cast-iron skillet over medium heat. While the pan is heating, chop 3 slices of the bacon. Add the chopped bacon and green onions to the pan and cook until the onions soften, about 5 minutes. Add the garlic and cook for another 2 minutes, until the garlic is fragrant and the bacon is browning. Remove the bacon mixture from the pan and set aside.

Add the butter to the skillet and cook the livers for about 4 minutes per side, working in batches if necessary. You want them browned on the outside but a little pink on the inside.

Transfer the livers and the bacon mixture to a food processor or high-powered blender. Add the shredded duck leg, figs, thyme, cloves, bloomed broth, and 1 teaspoon of salt. Pulse until the ingredients are combined but the mixture is not completely smooth.

Line a 9 by 5-inch loaf pan crosswise with the remaining bacon slices, overlapping them slightly and ensuring the strips hang over both sides of the pan. Scoop the blended mixture into the pan and smooth the top with a spatula if needed.

Fold over the bacon so it covers the top of the terrine. Cover with aluminum foil and place inside a larger baking pan with at least 3-inch-high sides. Fill the baking pan with enough warm water to come halfway up the sides of the loaf pan.

Carefully place the baking pan in the oven and bake for 2 hours. Remove the baking pan from the oven, then remove the loaf pan from the hot water bath and allow to cool for at least 20 minutes.

Remove the foil, replace with fresh foil or a lid, and transfer to the fridge to chill overnight or up to 24 hours before serving.

To make the blueberry sauce:

Just before serving, make the blueberry sauce: In a medium saucepan over medium heat, cook the blueberries and maple syrup for 10 to 15 minutes, stirring every few minutes to prevent sticking or burning on the bottom. The sauce is ready when the blueberries have softened and the liquid has reduced and become thicker. Just before removing from the heat, stir in the vanilla and salt. Let the sauce cool for 5 minutes before serving atop the terrine.

To serve, cut the terrine into slices and serve cold or room temperature with the blueberry sauce.

BACON LIVER BURGERS

YIELD: **4 servings**   PREP TIME: **20 minutes**   COOK TIME: **10 minutes**

Every parent knows that the best way to get kids to eat healthy is to hide the healthy stuff in something delicious—and what's more delicious than a burger? A great starting point for eating organ meats is to mix a bit of ground liver or heart into ground muscle meat when making things like burgers; stick to a 3:1 or 4:1 ratio of muscle meat to organ meat to ensure that the flavor and texture stay basically the same as a traditional burger. Of course, throwing some bacon in there too never hurts! I like to add sauerkraut and some sliced pepper Jack cheese to my lettuce-wrapped burger (a go-to "bun" for those sticking to Paleo or low-carb diets), but feel free to use whatever tasty condiments and wrappers or buns you like best.

2 pounds lean ground beef and beef liver mixture (see page 44)

8 ounces bacon, chopped

1 teaspoon coarse sea salt

1 teaspoon ground black pepper

¼ teaspoon ground cumin

¼ teaspoon garlic powder

¼ teaspoon onion powder

2 tablespoons bacon fat

Wraps or buns and burger fixings of choice

NOTE: *These burgers will keep for up to a week in the fridge or up to 3 weeks in the freezer; just defrost them in the fridge and then throw them back in a skillet to reheat.*

Put the ground beef and liver mixture, bacon, salt, and spices in a food processor or high-powered blender and pulse just until combined. The mixture will be slightly sticky. Using wet hands, shape into four 4-inch patties.

Heat the bacon fat in a 12-inch cast-iron skillet over medium-high heat. Add the patties and cook until they reach your desired doneness; I like to cook mine to medium, about 5 minutes per side.

Place each patty in the wrap or bun of your choice, then top with your preferred burger fixings and enjoy!

BEEFY BAKED MEATBALLS WITH CHÈVRE

YIELD: **4 servings**   PREP TIME: **30 minutes**   COOK TIME: **25 minutes**

This one's easy, because everyone loves meatballs, right? I try to make it a rule not to "hide" special ingredients like liver, brain, and heart because I want to normalize these highly nutritious and delicious foods, but that doesn't mean organ meat always has to be front and center. Sometimes it's okay to sneak in some healthier, slightly more challenging ingredients the way your parents may have sneaked broccoli under melted cheese or ground-up medicine into your yogurt. You may notice a slightly smoother texture, but most people won't taste the difference between these and their regular homemade meatballs, especially with that rich, creamy, melty goat cheese in the center. They go great with crispy air-fried sweet potato noodles, as well as conventional spaghetti, zoodles, cauliflower rice, roasted veggies, or some toasted garlic bread.

2 tablespoons extra-virgin olive oil

1 yellow onion, finely diced

½ cup finely chopped fresh parsley

1 pound lean ground beef and beef liver mixture (see page 44)

2 large eggs

1 tablespoon fine sea salt

1 teaspoon ground black pepper

½ teaspoon ground cumin

½ teaspoon smoked paprika

¼ teaspoon turmeric powder

8 ounces fresh (soft) goat cheese

Preheat the oven to 425°F. Line a rimmed baking sheet with parchment paper.

Heat the olive oil in a skillet over medium heat. Add the onion and sauté until softened but not browned, about 5 minutes. Transfer to a large bowl. Add the parsley to the bowl and allow the onion to cool.

To the bowl with the onion and parsley, add the ground meat mixture, eggs, salt, and spices and mix with your hands until combined.

Using wet hands, form the meat mixture into twelve 1½-inch balls (about the size of a golf ball). With clean hands, make an indentation in the center of each meatball. Put about a teaspoon of goat cheese in the indentation and seal.

Place the meatballs on the lined baking sheet so they are not touching. Bake until browned and cooked through in the center, about 20 minutes.

NOTES: *If you'd like to test the seasoning of the meat mixture before forming it into meatballs and baking them, take a small spoonful of the raw mixture, shape it into a small patty, and cook it in a skillet over medium heat. Remove from the pan and let cool, then taste to judge the seasoning. Add more salt and/or spices, if desired.*

These meatballs will keep for up to a week in the fridge or up to a month in the freezer.

BODYBUILDER PLATE: MIXED MEATS WITH RICE

YIELD: 4 servings   **PREP TIME: 25 minutes, plus 1 hour to soak livers**   **COOK TIME: 20 minutes**

This recipe is about as basic as it gets: it's my take on a fun, flavorful version of bodybuilder food, which is essentially protein, nonstarchy green vegetables, and a slow-digesting, filling carb (white rice). I was a competitive bodybuilder for a few years and a for-fun bodybuilder for many more. While a bodybuilding diet tends to be monotonous, super strict, and very low in fat, there are some basic tenets that I still adhere to: make high-quality protein the staple of every meal; add slow-digesting carbs that support your energy demands and that you tolerate and digest well; and throw in some green veggies for texture, flavor, and nutrients. This mixed-meat combo is much more fun than typical bodybuilder fare of skinless chicken breast, and it's higher in vitamins and minerals. And let's not forget the importance of spices in making healthy, "clean" food infinitely more interesting, so feel free to add any spices you like to this one.

1 pound precooked chicken or beef sausages

1 pound boneless, skinless chicken thighs

10 ounces calf or chicken livers, cleaned (see page 120)

1 pound asparagus

4 tablespoons extra-virgin olive oil, divided

1 teaspoon garlic powder

1 teaspoon onion powder

1 teaspoon ground black pepper

2 cups white rice

2 cups filtered water

2 cups beef or chicken bone broth (page 58 or 52)

Coarse sea salt, for finishing

2 lemon wedges, for finishing (optional)

Preheat the oven to 375°F. Line a rimmed baking sheet with parchment paper.

Cut the sausages into 1-inch pieces. Cut the chicken thighs into 1-inch cubes.

Pat the livers dry and cut them into 1-inch pieces.

Wash the asparagus, then snap off the woody ends.

In a large bowl, toss the sausages, chicken, and livers with 3 tablespoons of the olive oil until coated. Add the spices and stir to combine.

Spread the meat mixture in a single layer on the lined baking sheet, leaving some space on one side for the asparagus. Place the asparagus on the baking sheet and drizzle evenly with the remaining tablespoon of olive oil.

Bake for 20 minutes, until the chicken and livers are fully cooked and the asparagus is tender and beginning to brown. (When fully cooked, the livers will have become firm and turned a darker brown on the outside but should be a little pink in the middle.)

NOTES: *Cooking the rice in half bone broth (any of my recipes will do) and half water adds flavor and nutrition. If you don't have broth on hand, use 4 cups of filtered water.*

This meal will keep in the fridge for up to 3 days. If you really want to emulate bodybuilders, portion it out into separate storage containers so you don't have to measure—just pull out a container, reheat, and eat!

Meanwhile, cook the rice in a medium saucepan following the package instructions but using half water, half bone broth as the cooking liquid, which will make the rice more flavorful. Let sit for 10 minutes after cooking.

When the meats and asparagus are done, remove the pan from the oven. Place servings of rice on plates and top with the meat mixture and asparagus (or arrange as desired); finish with coarse sea salt and a squeeze of lemon juice, if desired, and serve hot.

FOIE GRAS PROFITEROLES

YIELD: **about 30 profiteroles**   PREP TIME: **40 minutes, plus 3 hours to chill filling**   COOK TIME: **45 minutes**

Beth Lipton is a health writer, speaker, health coach, and recipe developer (among many other skills and jobs), and a very good friend of mine. When I asked her to participate in my cookbook, she immediately recommended foie gras, and I was reminded, for the millionth time, why we get along so well! Foie gras is a French delicacy—it's the fattened liver of a duck, and it's incredibly rich and decadent. You can find whole foie gras at many butcher shops and specialty meat shops, as well as mousse or pâté made with foie gras. Here's Beth's story about this unique recipe:

"I first had foie gras donuts many years ago at Collicchio & Sons in New York City. It was especially memorable because in general I don't love either foie gras or donuts, but the combination was spectacular. When Ashleigh asked me to contribute an offal recipe, my brain went right to that sweet-savory combination. Instead of donuts, this version includes a spin on pâte à choux, *the dough traditional to éclairs and profiteroles. These unusual little puffs would make a great hors d'oeuvre for a party, or you could serve them for dessert if you and your guests like a savory twist on sweets. Make the fillings ahead of time, and don't let the pastry intimidate you—it's actually very simple and really fun if you like to nerd out a bit in the kitchen."*

BERRY JAM:

1 cup frozen raspberries, blueberries, strawberries, or a combination, thawed

Pinch of fine sea salt

2 tablespoons honey, preferably raw

2 tablespoons chia seeds

SPECIAL EQUIPMENT (recommended):

Stand mixer with paddle attachment

Piping bag

To make the jam:

Put the berries and salt in a medium saucepan. Cook over medium-low heat, stirring, until simmering and slightly thickened, 5 to 6 minutes. Remove from the heat.

Blend the berries in a blender or with an immersion blender until smooth; add the honey and blend for a few more seconds, then transfer to a medium bowl. Stir in the chia seeds. Taste and add more honey, if desired.

Cover and let cool; the jam will thicken as it cools.

FOIE GRAS FILLING:

8 ounces foie gras, chopped

1 shallot, finely chopped

1 tablespoon bourbon

¼ cup coconut cream

2 teaspoons grated orange zest

¼ teaspoon fine sea salt

To make the filling:

Put the foie gras in a medium skillet over low heat. Cook, stirring occasionally, until the fat renders, 2 to 4 minutes.

Add the shallot and cook, stirring occasionally, until the shallot and foie gras are very soft and the foie gras is beginning to darken in color, 4 to 5 minutes.

Add the bourbon and cook for 1 minute.

Transfer to a blender; let cool for a few minutes, then add the coconut cream, zest, and salt and blend until smooth and well combined. Transfer to a bowl, cover, and refrigerate until set, at least 3 hours.

PUFFS:

1 cup arrowroot powder

¼ cup blanched almond flour

3 tablespoons coconut sugar

¼ teaspoon fine sea salt

6 tablespoons unsalted grass-fed butter, cut into pieces

⅔ cup full-fat coconut milk

½ teaspoon vanilla extract

2 large eggs, at room temperature

NOTES: *If you have a stand mixer, I suggest you use it to beat the vanilla and eggs into the dough for the puffs; the process will be easier and quicker than if using a hand mixer. I use a hand mixer to make the choux dough, and it works fine; you simply need patience. Alternatively, if you have lots of patience and a strong arm, you can use a wooden spoon to beat the dough.*

You can make the jam and the foie gras filling up to 3 days ahead; keep both covered and refrigerated. Stir the foie gras filling to loosen before spreading.

To make the puffs:

Preheat the oven to 375°F and line a large baking sheet with parchment paper.

In a bowl, whisk together the arrowroot, almond flour, coconut sugar, and salt until well combined.

In a large saucepan over medium-low heat, combine the butter and coconut milk. Cook until the butter melts and the mixture comes to a low boil. Reduce the heat to low. Add the arrowroot mixture; stir well with a wooden spoon until a sticky dough forms and holds together in a ball.

Transfer the dough to a large mixing bowl; let cool until just warm to the touch. Don't worry if some of the fat separates; it will mix back in.

Using a hand mixer on medium speed (or a wooden spoon if working by hand), beat the vanilla into the dough.

Beat in 1 egg; as you beat, the mixture will separate and then come back together. When the mixture comes back together, beat in the remaining egg. Raise the speed to medium-high and beat until the dough is thickened and smooth and holds its shape.

Transfer the dough to a piping bag with a plain tip (or use a large zip-top bag; seal the bag, squeeze out the excess air, and snip off one corner). Pipe 1½- to 2-inch rounds onto the lined baking sheet. (Keep the fingers of one hand lightly moistened; when you've finished piping a puff, use moistened fingers to separate the puff from the pastry bag so you can move on to the next.)

Bake until the puffs are golden and firm, 20 to 22 minutes. (Do not open the oven door until at least 20 minutes have passed.) Using a paring knife, cut a slit in the side of each puff, then return the pan to the oven for 5 minutes more. Remove and transfer the puffs to a wire rack to cool completely.

When the puffs are completely cool, slice in half horizontally with a serrated knife; remove the tops. Pipe or spread 1 teaspoon of the foie gras filling on the bottom half of each and top with about 1 teaspoon of jam. Replace the tops and serve.

CHAPTER 7

LET'S GET GUTSY

GRILLED SWEETBREAD TACOS

YIELD: **8 tacos**   PREP TIME: **20 minutes, plus 12 hours to soak sweetbreads**   COOK TIME: **40 minutes**

Seattle-based gluten-free chef Nikki DeGidio is a woman after my own heart: she loves to eat, enjoys organ meats, and wants to balance the enjoyment of food with eating a nutritious diet. A longtime chef with a passion for pasta, she was forced to shift her entire culinary paradigm after a diagnosis of celiac disease diagnosis. Now, as a recipe developer, she offers gluten-free and whole-food options for those of us trying to optimize both the deliciousness and the nutritiousness of our meals. We met when she offered to host an event of mine at the former Lucky Santo, an incredible Seattle restaurant she opened to showcase how vibrant and tasty gluten-free and Paleo eating can be. Here's what Nikki had to say about her sweetbread taco recipe:

"Finally getting to work with sweetbreads again is such a treat! Despite this being a recipe for tacos, the use of sweetbreads brings me back to my French cooking roots. There are steps and procedures, but none of it complicated. Sweetbreads truly have a wonderful texture and flavor, and my hope is that this recipe demystifies one of the lesser known (even in the offal-eating community) cuts!"

TACOS:

2 pounds veal sweetbreads

2 cups beef or chicken bone broth (page 58 or 52) or vegetable stock

2 cups filtered water

Extra-virgin olive oil, for coating the sweetbreads

Fine sea salt

8 (6-inch) cassava or other grain-free tortillas (see Notes), warmed, or 8 large lettuce/cabbage leaves

1 cup shredded green cabbage

½ cup diced radishes

Fresh cilantro sprigs, for garnish

Lime wedges, for serving

QUICK PICKLED SHALLOTS WITH JALAPEÑO:

1 large shallot, or ½ small red onion

1 jalapeño pepper

About ½ cup red wine vinegar or apple cider vinegar

Splash of extra-virgin olive oil

PUMPKIN SEED SALSA VERDE:

1 bunch fresh parsley, leaves and stems

Grated zest and juice of 1 lime

¼ cup extra-virgin olive oil

1 tablespoon apple cider vinegar

1 small shallot, roughly chopped

2 cloves garlic, peeled

2 tablespoons raw pumpkin seeds

Fine sea salt (optional)

Soak the sweetbreads in salted water (use 1 teaspoon of salt for every 4 cups of water) in the refrigerator for 12 to 24 hours. The saltwater will draw out any lingering blood and impurities. At least 2 hours (and up to 6 hours) before you plan to make the tacos, prepare the picked shallots.

To make the pickled shallots:

Slice the shallot and jalapeño into ¼-inch rings and put them in a bowl or other storage container. Pour enough vinegar into the container to cover about three-quarters of the mixture, then add a splash of olive oil. Stir (or shake gently if the container has a tight-fitting lid) and let sit at room temperature for at least 2 hours or up to 6 hours before use.

When the sweetbreads are done soaking, thoroughly drain them. In a pot large enough to fit the sweetbreads comfortably in a single layer, heat the bone broth and water. When the liquid comes to a boil, turn the heat down to a simmer and slide the soaked and drained sweetbreads into the pot. Cover and simmer until tender, about 30 minutes. Meanwhile, make the salsa verde.

To make the salsa:

Put all the ingredients in a blender and blend until smooth. Season with salt, if desired.

To grill the sweetbreads and assemble the tacos:

After 30 minutes, remove the sweetbreads from the pot and discard the liquid. Allow the sweetbreads to cool until they're comfortable to handle. (*Tip:* To cool them quickly as well as firm them up and make them easier to work with, soak them in ice water for about 30 minutes, then drain.) Once the sweetbreads are cool, use your fingers to peel away any extra membrane and break them into thumb-size chunks; they will feel firm and break apart easily.

Preheat a barbecue grill to medium-high heat or preheat a grill pan on the stovetop over medium-high heat.

Toss the sweetbreads into a large bowl with enough olive oil to coat, then season with salt. Grill on all sides until they start to turn a bit crispy and golden, about 5 minutes per side.

Spoon a bit of the salsa into a tortilla or lettuce or cabbage leaf, followed by a generous pinch of shredded cabbage, then a few pieces of sweetbreads, some diced radish, a sprig of cilantro, and some pickled shallots with jalapeño. Serve with lime wedges.

SAUTÉED SWEETBREADS AND FIG SALAD

YIELD: **4 servings**   PREP TIME: **10 minutes, plus 1 hour to soak sweetbreads**   COOK TIME: **36 minutes**

The range of textures and flavors in this salad is highly sophisticated for such an easy recipe! Feel free to switch up the salad fixings, but I promise this is a salad that will leave you feeling satisfied.

SWEETBREADS:

1 pound lamb sweetbreads

½ teaspoon plus a pinch of fine sea salt, divided

2 cups filtered water

⅓ cup coconut flour

½ teaspoon ground black pepper

½ teaspoon paprika

3 tablespoons ghee

SALAD:

2 teaspoons balsamic vinegar

1 teaspoon honey, preferably raw

2 tablespoons extra-virgin olive oil

½ teaspoon fine sea salt

6 cups arugula

2 pears, sliced

½ cup dried figs, quartered

1 cucumber, sliced

4 ounces fresh (soft) goat cheese, crumbled

½ cup toasted unsalted walnut halves

To make the sweetbreads:

Gently rinse the sweetbreads and soak them in a bowl of cold filtered water with a pinch of salt for a minimum of 1 hour or up to 12 hours (overnight). Drain the sweetbreads.

In a pot large enough to fit the sweetbreads in a single layer, bring the water to a boil. Turn the heat down to maintain a simmer, add the sweetbreads, and simmer for about 30 minutes, until tender but solid to the touch; they should no longer be super soft and delicate-feeling, but firm without being rubbery. Remove the sweetbreads from the water and allow to cool. (*Tip:* To cool them quickly as well as firm them up and make them easier to work with, soak them in ice water for about 30 minutes, then drain.) Once the sweetbreads are cool, use your fingers to remove any visible membranes or fat. Break into 1-inch pieces.

In a medium bowl, mix the coconut flour with ¼ teaspoon of the salt, the pepper, and paprika. Dredge the sweetbread pieces in the flour mixture until covered.

In a 12-inch cast-iron skillet over medium-high heat, sauté the sweetbreads in the ghee until golden brown and crispy, about 3 minutes per side. When done, place on a paper towel–lined plate to drain.

To make the salad:

Make the dressing: Whisk together the balsamic vinegar, honey, olive oil, and salt in a small bowl.

Toss the arugula, pears, figs, and cucumber in a large bowl. Top with the goat cheese and walnuts. To serve, place 2 cups of salad in each of 4 large bowls, drizzle evenly with the dressing, and top with the warm sweetbreads.

NOTES: *Due to their delicate, creamy nature, sweetbreads are best eaten right after cooking; however, they will keep for up to 3 days in the fridge. You can reheat them in a skillet over medium heat with another tablespoon of ghee for about 5 minutes.*

The salad fixings, if not dressed, will keep for up to 5 days in the fridge.

EASY GRILLED SWEETBREADS

YIELD: **4 servings**   PREP TIME: **10 minutes, plus 1 hour to soak sweetbreads**   COOK TIME: **37 minutes**

Sweetbreads are so delicious, even people who wouldn't normally eat "adventurous" cuts love them, which is why they end up on so many restaurant menus. Sweetbreads are most often prepared breaded and fried, but in this simple grilled preparation they develop a nice crust on the outside while staying rich and creamy on the inside. Since they're delicate, you have to be a little more careful about how you prepare them than other, heartier cuts (like heart), but the work is absolutely worth it. They truly don't need to be dressed up with fancy sides, although a flavorful dipping sauce is always welcome; I particularly enjoy something tart or acidic to balance the mild creaminess of the meat, such as the Chimichurri Dipping Sauce on page 220.

1 pound lamb or veal sweetbreads

2 cups filtered water, plus more for soaking

1 teaspoon plus 1 pinch fine ground salt, divided

4 tablespoons extra-virgin olive oil, divided

1 tablespoon coconut aminos or balsamic vinegar

½ teaspoon ground black pepper

SPECIAL EQUIPMENT:

4 (9-inch) wood skewers, soaked in water for 1 hour

NOTE: *The sweetbreads will keep in the fridge for up to 3 days, but I recommend you eat them right away. You can reheat them on the stovetop, in a pan over medium heat with another tablespoon of ghee for about 5 minutes.*

Gently rinse the sweetbreads and soak them in a bowl of cold filtered water with a pinch of salt for a minimum of 1 hour or up to 12 hours (overnight). Drain the sweetbreads.

In a pot large enough to fit the sweetbreads in a single layer, bring 2 cups of filtered water to a boil. Turn the heat down to maintain a simmer, add the sweetbreads, and simmer for about 30 minutes, until firm but not rubbery. Remove the sweetbreads from the water and put them in a large bowl of ice water, which will allow them to cool and firm up for the grill.

Pat the sweetbreads dry with a paper towel and, with your fingers, remove any visible membranes or fat. Separate into roughly 1½-inch pieces using your fingers. (Even when cooked, they're delicate and will break apart easily, so make sure you don't mush them up too much!)

Put the sweetbreads in a large bowl and toss with 2 tablespoons of the olive oil, the coconut aminos, the remaining teaspoon of salt, and the pepper. Then thread the sweetbread pieces carefully onto the skewers, about 5 pieces per skewer.

Heat the remaining 2 tablespoons of oil in a large grill pan over medium heat.

Grill the sweetbreads on the grill pan, turning occasionally, until golden brown on all sides, about 7 minutes total. Transfer to a platter and let stand for 5 minutes before serving.

CRISPY FRIED KIDNEY

YIELD: **4 servings**   PREP TIME: **10 minutes, plus 1 hour to soak kidney**   COOK TIME: **10 minutes**

This easy and tasty recipe comes from my friends at Crowd Cow, a Seattle-based meat subscription company. The owners wrote an incredible book called *Craft Beef* that really tells the story of beef: how to raise and harvest it sustainably, how to enjoy all aspects of the animal, and why treating our food with reverence and respect is a beautiful and important thing.

1 beef kidney (about 1 pound), cleaned and prepped (see below)

4 tablespoons extra-virgin olive oil, divided

1 cup blanched almond or cassava flour

1 tablespoon fine sea salt

1 tablespoon ground black pepper

2 tablespoons unsalted grass-fed butter

3 cloves garlic, minced

2 teaspoons ground coriander

1 tablespoon fresh lemon juice

Pat the kidney dry and cut it into 1-inch cubes. Toss in a medium bowl with 2 tablespoons of the olive oil until well coated.

In another medium bowl, combine the flour, salt, and pepper. Dredge the kidney pieces well in the flour mixture.

Heat the remaining 2 tablespoons of oil in a 12-inch cast-iron skillet over high heat. When the oil is hot, add the kidney cubes and fry until cooked through, about 7 minutes. Remove the kidney from the pan and place on a plate lined with a paper towel to soak up any excess oil.

In the same pan, melt the butter, then add the garlic and coriander and cook until the garlic turns light brown. Return the kidney to the pan, then add the lemon juice. Cook for 30 more seconds and finish with a liberal sprinkle of salt and pepper.

NOTES: *Because beef kidneys tend to have a stronger flavor than the kidneys of smaller animals, it's key to soak them to remove impurities, as instructed. Consider serving these with a tasty dipping sauce, like the Lemon Garlic Dipping Sauce on page 222. If you're hesitant about stronger-tasting offal, start with smaller kidneys, such as veal or lamb, before working your way up to the big show! This will keep in the fridge for about 4 days.*

How to Clean and Prep Kidneys

To prepare kidneys for cooking, begin by removing any outer fat or membranes. Then cut the kidneys in half lengthwise and remove the tough white gristle from the inside. Once this is done, rinse in cold water and, to reduce some of the stronger flavor of the kidney, soak in cold water with a pinch of salt and 1 tablespoon of apple cider vinegar (or the juice of 1 lemon) for 1 hour. Drain, pat dry with a paper towel, and proceed with the recipe as written.

SAUTÉED VEAL KIDNEYS WITH GARLIC AND ONION

YIELD: **4 servings**   PREP TIME: **5 minutes, plus 1 hour to soak kidneys**   COOK TIME: **16 minutes**

A quick sauté (rather than a long, slow braise) is great for small kidneys like veal and lamb. This dish works well as an entrée next to a salad or roasted vegetables.

2 cloves garlic, minced

2 tablespoons unsalted grass-fed butter

1 large white onion, sliced

1 pound veal or lamb kidneys, cleaned and prepped (see page 152)

¼ cup dry white wine

1 sprig fresh parsley, finely chopped

Coarse sea salt and ground black pepper

NOTE: *While the sautéed kidneys will keep in the fridge for up to 3 days, it's best to eat this dish hot and fresh!*

In a large skillet, sauté the garlic in the butter over medium heat until just turning brown around the edges, about 4 minutes. Add the onion and cook until it softens and begins to caramelize, about 4 minutes. Meanwhile, cut the kidneys into ½-inch cubes.

Raise the heat to high and add the kidney pieces. Sauté until browned, about 5 minutes. Add the wine and stir to deglaze the pan, then cook for another 3 minutes. The kidneys should be faintly pink on the inside; if you overcook them, they will become tough.

Transfer the kidney and onion mixture to a serving dish. Mix in the parsley, season with salt and pepper, and serve.

CONFIT CHICKEN GIZZARDS

YIELD: **4 servings** PREP TIME: **5 minutes, plus time to marinate overnight** COOK TIME: **2½ hours**

If you want to make something rich and decadent, confit is the answer—especially with duck fat, one of the richest and most delicious cooking fats on the planet! These rich morsels work wonderfully on a light salad or atop a bed of rice or couscous, or with my Duck Fat–Fried Potatoes on page 230.

1 pound chicken gizzards, cleaned (see Notes)

4 cloves garlic, roughly chopped

4 sprigs fresh thyme

1 teaspoon coarse sea salt

1 teaspoon ground black pepper

1½ cups duck fat, melted

Preheat the oven to 325°F.

Put the gizzards in a 6 by 8-inch baking dish. Add the garlic, thyme, salt, and pepper and mix, then add the duck fat and mix again until the gizzards are evenly coated. Cover with aluminum foil and bake for 2½ hours.

Remove from the oven and drain the gizzards in a fine-mesh strainer. Store the strained duck fat in a separate container in the refrigerator to use for other cooking.

Serve the gizzards hot, either whole or thinly sliced.

NOTES: *Gizzards aren't too intimating to look at or handle; they're like little bits of dark meat. When you purchase gizzards, they will likely be prepared for you: that is, cut open and cleaned of inner grit. They should be a deep, rich red color, with a clean, meaty smell. Gizzards may have some visible outer fat or connective tissue; simply remove it with a small paring knife.*

The cooked gizzards will keep in the fridge for up to a week, the duck fat for up to 6 months. To reheat the gizzards, pan-fry them in a little of the leftover fat over medium heat until warmed through.

KIDNEY KEBABS WITH MINT TABBOULEH

YIELD: **6 servings**   PREP TIME: **10 minutes, plus 1 hour to season kidneys**   COOK TIME: **10 minutes**

There is a small but vibrant Lebanese community in Nova Scotia, the maritime province of Canada where I grew up, so I like to think I have a bit of familiarity with the delicious flavors and textures of Lebanese food. I wanted to include a tabbouleh recipe in this book because it's one of the rare instances where a purely vegetarian component of a meal has the opportunity to outshine its meaty counterpart! Tabbouleh is essentially a chopped parsley salad, but with the right amount of herbs and citrus, it makes for an incredibly bright and flavorful addition that steals the show— and just might subdue some of the stronger flavors in the beef kidney. In this recipe, I left out the bulgur wheat that is typically included and added mint because, while bulgur does add a bit of texture and chew, I really don't think it's necessary, and the tabbouleh is a little healthier this way.

KIDNEY KEBABS:

1 beef kidney (about 1 pound), cleaned and prepped (see page 152)

1 teaspoon smoked paprika

1 teaspoon ground cumin

1 teaspoon fine sea salt

TABBOULEH:

1 medium tomato, finely chopped

1 small cucumber, finely chopped

4 green onions, finely chopped

1 cup finely chopped fresh parsley

⅓ cup finely chopped fresh mint

1 cup finely chopped pistachios

3 tablespoons fresh lime juice

3 tablespoons extra-virgin olive oil

Coarse sea salt

SPECIAL EQUIPMENT:

6 (9-inch) wood skewers, soaked in water for 1 hour

To season the kidney:

Cut the kidney into ½-inch cubes.

In a small bowl, combine the spices and salt and massage onto the meat cubes with your hands. Cover and place in the fridge to season for a minimum of 1 hour or up to overnight. About 30 minutes before you plan to grill the kidney kebabs, make the tabbouleh.

To make the tabbouleh:

Put the tomato in a colander to drain the excess juice. Combine the rest of the vegetables, the herbs, and pistachios in a medium bowl, then add the drained tomatoes.

Add the lime juice, olive oil, and salt to taste and mix. Cover and refrigerate for 30 minutes.

NOTES: *If you're a bread person, some pita would be a great addition this meal—just throw the tabbouleh on your pita, add a couple pieces of hot grilled kidney, and dig in!*

The tabbouleh should keep in the fridge for up to 4 days; after that, it'll start to get soggy. I recommend you eat the kidney within 2 days.

To grill the kebabs:

Preheat a barbecue grill to medium heat or preheat a grill pan on the stovetop over medium heat. Thread the seasoned kidney cubes onto the skewers, about 5 pieces per skewer.

Grill the kebabs for 8 to 10 minutes, rotating every 3 or 4 minutes, until browned. The meat should be firm on the outside but still relatively soft (not raw) on the inside. Do not overcook, or the meat will be rubbery.

To serve, divide the tabbouleh among 6 plates. Place a kebab on top, or take the meat off the stick and place the pieces on top of the tabbouleh.

WARM POTATO SALAD WITH TRIPE

YIELD: **4 to 6 servings (as an appetizer or side dish)**   PREP TIME: **30 minutes**   COOK TIME: **3 hours**

Everyone likes potato salad, right? In this warm preparation, tripe adds visual interest and a chewy, meaty texture. (In this type of potato salad, it's usually bacon that supplies the latter.) Tripe's fairly mild flavor is easily subsumed by the punchy vinegar dressing and hit of chili flakes in this recipe. This unique take on potato salad would taste fantastic next to a steak or roast chicken.

1 pound beef tripe, cleaned (see sidebar, opposite)

Filtered water

1 medium yellow onion, roughly chopped

6 garlic cloves, minced

1 tablespoon fresh thyme leaves, or 1½ teaspoons dried

2 bay leaves

1 tablespoon fine sea salt

½ cup dry white wine

1 tablespoon red wine vinegar

1 pound fingerling or other small potatoes

3 tablespoons duck or bacon fat, if pan-frying the potatoes

Dried rosemary leaves, for garnish (optional)

VINAIGRETTE:

½ cup extra-virgin olive oil

2 tablespoons red wine vinegar

1 tablespoon fresh lemon juice

½ cup fresh parsley leaves, finely chopped

1 teaspoon red pepper flakes

Fine sea salt

SPECIAL EQUIPMENT (recommended):

Air fryer

Put the cleaned tripe in a stockpot and cover with about 2 quarts of filtered water. Add the onion, garlic, thyme, bay leaves, salt, wine, and red wine vinegar. Bring to a boil, then reduce the heat and simmer uncovered until the tripe is very tender, about 3 hours. Skim off any scum that rises to the surface. Remove the pot from the heat and let the tripe cool in the cooking liquid.

Meanwhile, slice the potatoes lengthwise, about ½ inch thick, or cut into ½-inch thick rounds. Air-fry the potatoes, or pan-fry them in a 12-inch cast-iron skillet in the fat, until they're easily pierced with a paring knife and browned and crispy on the outside, about 10 minutes. Set aside in a large bowl.

Make the vinaigrette: In a separate bowl, combine the olive oil, red wine vinegar, lemon juice, parsley, and red pepper flakes. Season to taste with salt and whisk until mixed.

When the tripe is cool, thinly slice into ribbons and add to the bowl with the potatoes.

Toss the potatoes and tripe with the vinaigrette and serve immediately. Sprinkle with dried rosemary, if desired.

How to Clean Beef Tripe

Most beef tripe sourced from a butcher will already be cleaned, but since tripe is essentially the animal's stomach lining, you want to make sure; it's best to thoroughly rinse it yourself until any visible impurities are removed.

To clean the tripe, lay it on a cutting board and, using a sharp knife, scrape away any visible fat or dirt. Next, par-boil the tripe for 10 minutes in salted boiling water, then remove and rinse in cold water; at this point, the tripe should look clean. Once it's been boiled and cooled and is free of any visible impurities, it's ready to use in the recipe as directed.

BAKED TRIPE WITH ZUCCHINI FRIES

YIELD: **4 servings**   PREP TIME: **20 minutes**   COOK TIME: **30 minutes**

If you want to experiment with a new ingredient but you're a little scared, what better first step is there than to bread it? Breading anything makes it more delicious—it's science—and tripe is no exception. Its fibrous, chewy texture requires long, slow cooking, and that's actually part of the fun. This easy and comforting dish works perfectly with my Lemon Garlic Dipping Sauce on page 222. Zucchini fries are a lower-carb take on regular fries, and the tripe is mild and chewy, like breaded calamari!

Coconut or avocado oil cooking spray

8 ounces zucchini

1 cup blanched almond flour or gluten-free baking flour blend

½ teaspoon fine sea salt

½ teaspoon ground black pepper

2 large eggs

1 pound beef tripe, cleaned (see page 159)

Fresh lemon juice, for finishing

NOTE: *As with all fried dishes, this one is best eaten hot and fresh, but you can store leftovers in the fridge for up to 2 days. To reheat, toss in an air fryer for about 5 minutes or in a skillet over medium heat with a bit of ghee or butter until warmed.*

Preheat the oven to 425°F. Line 2 rimmed baking sheets with parchment paper and spray lightly with cooking spray.

Slice the zucchini into ½-inch-wide strips; you want them to look like French fries.

In a dish or small bowl, mix the flour with the salt and pepper for dredging.

Crack the eggs into a medium bowl and whisk. Toss the zucchini strips in the eggs a few at a time, then dredge in the flour mixture and place on one of the lined baking sheets so they aren't overlapping. Bake for 30 minutes.

Meanwhile, cut the cleaned tripe into ¼-inch-thick strips. Dredge the pieces of tripe in the egg mixture, then in the flour mixture and place on the second lined baking sheet.

After the zucchini fries have been in the oven for 20 minutes, place the pan of breaded tripe in the oven. Let both pans bake for 10 more minutes, until the tripe strips are beginning to brown and crisp. Remove the pans from the oven and serve the tripe and zucchini fries hot with a squeeze of lemon juice.

PORTUGUESE RED WINE TRIPE STEW

YIELD: **4 servings**   PREP TIME: **10 minutes**   COOK TIME: **2 hours**

The cozy, rich feeling (and many ingredients) of this dish was inspired by a meal I found myself eating often when I lived in Bermuda: *polvo guisado,* a traditional Azorean Portuguese octopus and red wine stew that is popular with the large Portuguese community there. It was so rich and seasoned so perfectly, and I loved the combination of the rich broth, chewy octopus, and starchy potato. I decided to switch out octopus for chewy tripe and potato for starchy chickpeas, and here we are: another hearty, warming, unique mouthful.

1 pound beef tripe, cleaned (see page 159)

1 small white onion, finely chopped

3 cloves garlic, minced

5 tablespoons extra-virgin olive oil, plus more for finishing

1 (6-ounce) can tomato paste

1 teaspoon paprika

1 teaspoon fine sea salt, plus more for finishing

¼ teaspoon ground black pepper, plus more for finishing

3 cups red wine, divided

2 cups filtered water, divided

2 bay leaves

1 (15-ounce) can chickpeas

8 ounces Spanish-style dry-cured chorizo, chopped

NOTE: *This stew will keep for up to a week in the fridge or up to a month in the freezer.*

Cut the cleaned tripe into 1-inch pieces and set aside.

In a large stockpot over medium heat, sauté the onion and garlic in the olive oil until the onion has softened.

Add the tripe, tomato paste, paprika, salt, and pepper and stir.

Pour in 2 cups of the wine and 1 cup of the water. Stir and bring to a low simmer. Cover the pot, reduce the heat to medium-low, and simmer for about 1 hour, stirring occasionally so the stew doesn't burn on the bottom and sides.

After an hour, add the remaining cup of wine, the remaining cup of water, the bay leaves, and chickpeas and continue to simmer over low heat for another hour, until the chickpeas are softened but not mushy.

With about 10 minutes to go, stir in the chorizo to allow the flavors to infuse.

Ladle the stew into bowls, top with a bit more salt, pepper, and olive oil, and serve.

CHAPTER 8

BITS AND PIECES

SAVORY BLOOD PUDDING

YIELD: **12 servings**   PREP TIME: **20 minutes, plus time to set overnight**   COOK TIME: **1 hour 6 minutes**

This is hearty food: the kind you eat before going outdoors in the bracing Scottish Highlands to work with your hands. Most of us aren't doing that, perhaps, but the key here is that this is a highly caloric and nutritionally dense food that you can feel nourishing you as you eat it. Savory blood pudding is, of course, a pretty classic dish; you've probably heard of it even if you haven't tried it. I don't want to mess with something that's worked for centuries in the UK and Ireland, although I did make a few changes by keeping the onions and bacon roughly chopped for some texture and setting the pudding as more of a loaf cake than a sausage.

Traditionally, a savory "cake" or sausage made with blood was simply another way to get protein and nourishment cheaply and easily, as there was always plenty of blood available during the slaughter or harvest of an animal (and not always a lot of ways to store or refrigerate it). Most blood puddings are made with a base of blood, fat, and some kind of grain, like oats. Today, it's quite difficult to source fresh blood, so a lot of people aren't exposed to this delicacy, much less able to make it at home. Since I spend most of my time in a French-speaking part of Canada, I'm fortunate enough to be able to find *boudin noir,* or blood pudding, at a few local butcher shops and groceries and even source blood to make it at home. Depending on where you live, this may be a tricky ingredient to track down—but it's worth the work! This recipe essentially results in a meat cake that you can cut into thick slices and serve as is on a charcuterie plate (see page 178) or pan-fry, as here. Although pan-fried is my favorite way to enjoy this dish, you'll find that no matter how you serve it, it's creamy, rich, and not as minerally as you'd think; you won't feel like you're eating blood. Rather, you'll feel like you're eating something densely nutritious and rich in history and culture, and what's more nourishing than that?

1½ cups fresh beef or pork blood

2 teaspoons fine sea salt, divided

½ cup blanched almond flour or gluten-free baking flour blend

½ cup gluten-free oat flour

8 ounces bacon, roughly chopped (about 1 cup)

1 small white or yellow onion, roughly chopped

½ cup whole milk

1 teaspoon ground black pepper

½ teaspoon ground allspice

¼ teaspoon ground cinnamon

Ghee or bacon fat, for the pan

Preheat the oven to 325°F.

Pour the blood into a medium bowl and stir in 1 teaspoon of the salt; let sit for 10 minutes.

Line an 8½ by 4½-inch loaf pan with parchment paper, allowing some of the paper to hang over the sides.

NOTE: *Ask your local butcher if they can source safe, fresh blood, or ask at your local Asian markets. Since this is a more loose, fresh version of blood pudding (versus the more processed, dried or salted sausage version), you'll need to keep it in the fridge and consume it within a week, or freeze it for up to a month.*

Strain the blood with a fine-mesh strainer into a large bowl. Add the rest of the ingredients, except the ghee, and mix with a spoon until well combined. The mixture will be watery rather than doughy or thick.

Transfer the blood mixture to the lined loaf pan and cover with aluminum foil. Bake for 55 minutes, then remove the foil and bake uncovered for an additional 5 minutes to brown and crisp the top. When the pudding is done, a toothpick inserted in the middle should come out clean. Remove from the oven and allow to cool completely, about 30 minutes, before covering and placing in the fridge to set overnight.

When ready to serve, heat the ghee in a medium skillet over medium-high heat.

Cut the pudding into ½-inch-thick slices and pan-fry until browned and crispy, about 3 minutes per side. Serve immediately.

OFFAL OMELET

YIELD: **2 servings**   PREP TIME: **10 minutes**   COOK TIME: **15 minutes**

Omelets are one of the most filling and satisfying breakfast-or-anytime meals; you can add any ingredients you like, from fresh herbs and chopped vegetables to meat of any kind. As with any egg-based dish, it's better to make this omelet when you're prepared to eat it; it would taste great alongside my Duck Fat–Fried Potatoes on page 230. Think of this as a supercharged diner omelet!

1 cup finely diced button mushrooms

1 small white or yellow onion, finely diced

2 tablespoons unsalted grass-fed butter, divided

4 ounces lean ground beef and organ meat mixture (such as liver, heart, and/or kidney) (see page 44)

4 large eggs

½ cup shredded cheddar or pepper Jack cheese, plus more for garnish if desired

Pinch of fine sea salt

Coconut or avocado oil cooking spray

Sliced fresh chives, for garnish (optional)

Coarse sea salt and ground black pepper, for garnish (optional)

In a 12-inch cast-iron skillet over medium heat, sauté the mushrooms and onion in 1 tablespoon of the butter until soft, about 5 minutes. Remove from the pan and put in a medium bowl.

Add the remaining tablespoon of butter to the skillet and cook the ground meat mixture until browned, about 5 minutes. Add the cooked meat to the bowl with the mushrooms and onion and stir to combine. Set aside.

In a separate medium bowl, beat the eggs. Stir in the cheese and a pinch of salt.

Heat an 8-inch nonstick skillet over medium heat and coat with cooking spray. Pour in half of the egg mixture. As it begins to set around the edge of the pan, gently tilt the skillet to allow the uncooked egg to flow into the empty spaces and begin to set.

When the eggs are almost set on the surface but still look slightly wet, cover half of the omelet with half of the meat and veggie filling. Slip a silicone spatula under the unfilled side and fold the omelet over onto the filled half.

Cook for another minute, then slide the omelet onto a plate. Repeat the process for the second omelet.

Finish the omelets with more shredded cheese, chives, and coarse salt and pepper, if desired.

CHICKEN SKIN CHIPS

YIELD: **4 servings**   PREP TIME: **5 minutes**   COOK TIME: **30 minutes**

A friend of mine serves fried chicken skin as an appetizer at his restaurant, and the first time I tried it, I couldn't get over how simple and delicious it was. He mentioned that the dish is perfect for his clients and the restaurant: crunchy, salty, and delicious, it makes an awesome snack with a beer, and it is an easy and inexpensive offering for the restaurant since they can buy unwanted (unwanted?!?) chicken skin from the butcher for virtually nothing and make a great profit even with a reasonably priced appetizer. I don't think I'm even mildly exaggerating when I say that people who don't eat chicken skin are missing out on one of the greatest culinary pleasures in the universe.

Cleaned skin from 1 chicken (see Notes)

1½ teaspoons coarse sea salt

½ teaspoon ground black pepper

½ teaspoon paprika

NOTES: *This snack is great for keto, Paleo, and low-carb eaters, and it's surprisingly easy to prepare. Of course, you can add whatever spices you'd like to your chips; you can also toss them in your favorite hot sauce or even add some shredded cheese and veggies for chicken skin nachos!*

Most butcher shops should be able to provide you with chicken skin; once you get it home, all you need to do is to rinse it thoroughly in cold water, pat it dry, and, using a sharp paring knife, remove any remaining fat from the inside of the skin.

The chips will keep for a couple days in an airtight container at room temperature but are best eaten right away, as skin is delicate and, without preservatives, the chips are likely to become stale or go soft pretty quickly.

Preheat the oven to 350°F. Line a rimmed baking sheet with parchment paper.

Using sharp scissors, cut the chicken skin into 5 or 6 pieces. Bring a medium pot of water to a low boil. Using tongs, blanch each piece of chicken skin for a few seconds; you'll see the skin go from limp and white to slightly more firm or jellylike and translucent in color.

Place the skins in a fine-mesh strainer to drain, then pat dry between paper towels. Using the scissors, snip the skin into smaller, chip-sized pieces. Lay the pieces flat on a wire rack set on the lined baking sheet; this will allow air to flow above and below the chips so they crisp up nicely. Sprinkle with the salt, pepper, and paprika.

Bake until crispy, about 25 minutes; watch carefully to prevent it from burning.

Remove the pan from the oven. If you'd like your chips extra crispy, throw them into an air fryer at 350°F for about 5 minutes, watching to make sure they don't burn.

Remove to a medium heat-safe bowl, toss with more spices as desired, and serve hot and crispy.

CRISPY SALMON SKIN SALAD

YIELD: **2 servings**   PREP TIME: **10 minutes**   COOK TIME: **8 minutes**

From the discussion of collagen powder on pages 32 and 33, we know that fish skin is nutrient-packed, full of collagen and vitamins. What many people who automatically remove the skin from their fish don't know is that it's also by far the most delicious part of the fish! When cooked in fat, the skin is crispy, fatty, and full of flavor; I'm always stealing my friends' fish skin off of their plates if they're silly enough to skip it. I figured salmon salad is a pretty popular dish, so why not get right to the best part and make that crispy skin the highlight?

1 tablespoon ghee or unsalted grass-fed butter

4 (4-ounce) salmon fillets

Pinch of chopped fresh dill or dried dill weed

Pinch of coarse sea salt

6 cups mixed greens

½ cup dried cranberries

2 ounces fresh (soft) goat cheese, crumbled

2 ounces toasted and salted shelled sunflower seeds

3 tablespoons The Easiest Salad Dressing Ever (page 224), for finishing

NOTE: *Feel free to use the fish flesh in your salad too, but in the spirit of highlighting organs, I kept this recipe to skin only. We all know that salad doesn't keep well—it tends to get soggy once dressed—so I recommend eating this meal right after you make it.*

Heat the ghee in a cast-iron skillet over medium-high heat.

Pat the salmon dry with a paper towel and season both sides of the fillets with the dill and salt.

Once the skillet is hot, place the salmon fillets flesh side down in the pan and cook for about 3 minutes, then flip over onto the skin side and cook for another 4 to 5 minutes, until the salmon is fully cooked and the skin is crispy. (It's important that the skin gets crispy, so if you are worried about overcooking the salmon, you can remove the fillets from the skillet, carefully remove the skin from the flesh with a paring knife, and then return the skin to the skillet to continue crisping.)

Remove the salmon from the skillet and place on a plate to cool while you prep the salad.

Toss the greens, dried cranberries, goat cheese, and sunflower seeds together in a large bowl, then add the salad dressing and toss to coat.

Remove the salmon skin from the flesh (this task should be easy if the skin is crispy) and place the skin on top of salad to serve. (Alternatively, you can crumble up the crispy skin and toss it with the salad for a crunchy texture throughout.) Of course, you should save the flesh for another meal!

OXTAIL STEW

YIELD: 4 servings   PREP TIME: 10 minutes   COOK TIME: 3 hours 12 minutes

Since this book is about nose-to-tail eating, I had to include a recipe for tail, specifically oxtail—the type of tail most commonly used in cooking. While oxtail-based dishes are pretty popular in many parts of the world, from the Philippines and Jamaica to Africa and beyond, it's not exactly the most common cut of meat you'd buy at a grocery store in the United States. But oxtail can be found at butcher shops and markets catering to African, Asian, and Caribbean cuisine and from some online purveyors (see page 251). A surprisingly versatile and delicious cut composed of skin, cartilage, and a fair bit of muscle meat and fat, oxtail can be pickled, barbecued, boiled, or smoked—or, as in this recipe, made into a stew.

If you'd like a less messy dining experience, you can remove the cooked oxtails from the stew, cut the meat off the bones, and return the meat to the stew before serving, but I prefer to keep the bone in and eat with my hands! I've never heard anyone try oxtail and not rave about the rich, concentrated flavor—this is one of the truly meatiest mouthfuls around. Oxtails are rich in collagen, so cooking them down with the bone in results in a beautifully thick, hearty sauce. You're probably going to want some crusty bread (or maybe my collagen-rich beauty bread on page 206) to dip into this stew!

2 tablespoons bacon fat or unsalted grass-fed butter

3 pounds oxtails

Coarse sea salt and ground black pepper

1 large yellow onion, chopped

3 carrots, peeled and chopped into 1-inch pieces

4 cups beef bone broth (page 58)

2 cups dry red wine

3 cloves garlic, chopped

1 teaspoon dried thyme leaves

NOTE: *This stew will keep for up to a week in the fridge. You may notice a layer of hardened fat on top, which you can remove or stir back into the stew after you reheat it.*

Melt the fat in a large soup pot over medium-high heat.

Generously season the oxtails with salt and pepper, then add them to the pot (work in batches if necessary to avoid crowding) and sear on all sides, about 2 minutes per side. Place the seared pieces on a plate and set aside.

Reduce the heat to medium-low and add the chopped onion and carrots. Cook, stirring frequently so they don't burn or stick to the bottom of the pot, until the onion is soft and translucent, about 5 minutes.

Put the oxtails back in the pot and add the bone broth, wine, garlic, thyme, and 1 teaspoon of salt.

Cover and simmer for a total of 3 hours, or until the meat is fork-tender. During the first 2½ hours of cooking, check every 30 minutes or so to make sure the liquid isn't evaporating below the oxtails; if it is, add enough filtered water to cover the oxtails. Uncover the pot for the last half hour to allow the liquid to reduce to a thick, soupy broth. Before serving, taste and season with additional salt and pepper, if desired.

PORKY TRAIL MIX

YIELD: **8 servings**   PREP TIME: **5 minutes**   COOK TIME: **30 minutes**

Sticking to the golden rule that pork makes everything more delicious, think of this as a high-fat, highly delicious trail mix for your next road trip or hike, or the perfect bar snack—this fatty, sweet, slightly spicy, and salty combo is perfect with a beer. I'm always a fan of combining salty and sweet, and I think pork is complemented so well by both flavors, but if you want it sweeter, simply omit the cayenne; if you want it less sweet, skip the cinnamon and add some garlic powder instead.

8 ounces pig skin, cleaned and prepped (see below)

1 large egg white

2 tablespoons honey (preferably raw) or maple syrup

1 teaspoon coarse sea salt

1 teaspoon ground cinnamon

½ teaspoon cayenne pepper

8 ounces raw cashews

8 ounces raw pecans

4 ounces shelled raw pumpkin or sunflower seeds

Preheat the oven to 300°F. Line a rimmed baking sheet with parchment paper.

Pat the pig skin dry and cut into roughly ¾-inch pieces.

In a large bowl, whisk together the egg white, honey, salt, and spices. Toss in the nuts and pig skin pieces, making sure they're well coated.

Transfer the mixture to the lined baking sheet and spread it in a single layer.

Bake for about 30 minutes, until the pig skin pieces are golden brown and crunchy, rotating the pan halfway through. Pay attention so the skin doesn't burn!

How to Clean and Prep Pig Skin

With a sharp knife or kitchen shears, cut the skin into strips about 2 inches wide; this makes it easier to remove the excess fat. Using a sharp knife, score the fat on each strip about every 2 inches and then slice off the thick layer of fat as best you can. It's okay if you don't get it all; the key here is to get rid of as much fat as you can.

Put the pig skin strips in a large pot and cover with water. Bring the water to a low boil and continue to simmer for 1 hour, until the skin is translucent.

Carefully remove the skin with a slotted spoon and lay it flat on a cooling rack set on top of a rimmed baking sheet to catch any drips; discard the cooking water. Place the rack in the fridge and allow the skin to cool and dry out for a minimum of 2 hours or up to overnight.

Using a sharp knife or scraping implement, remove the rest of the fat from the underside of the cooled skin; it should come off relatively easily. If it still has a thin layer of fat, that's fine. At this point, you can proceed with the recipe as written.

NOTE: *Feel free to play with the spices and nut combos—there's no wrong choice! If you want it extra crispy, throw the mix into an air fryer at 400°F for a few minutes after baking.*

This mix is best served fresh and warm but will keep in an airtight container at room temperature for up to 2 days or in the fridge for up to 4 days. (The addition of pig skin means this trail mix won't stay fresh long.) If refrigerated, you can toss the mix in an air fryer for a few minutes to reheat it, or just let it come to room temperature.

THIS CHARCUTERIE PLATE IS OFFAL

YIELD: **Variable**   PREP TIME: **10 minutes**

Get creative with this one! This beautiful, fun spread is a culmination of all the hard work we've done throughout this cookbook, and it's a great way to introduce friends or family to some tasty organ meat snacks in a familiar setting. Everyone loves a charcuterie board! Add some pickled veggies, crusty bread and crackers, stone-ground mustard, and sweet jam or marmalade, and your dinner guests might forget that they're enjoying liver pâté and heart jerky. Or, even better, they might warm up to the idea quicker than you think.

Beef Heart Jerky (page 114)

Chicken Liver Mousse (page 126)

Savory Blood Pudding (page 166)

Chicken Skin Chips (page 170)

Plantain Chips (page 214)

Porky Trail Mix (page 176)

Sea Salt Paleo Crackers (page 210)

Bourbon Bacon Jam (page 216)

Grab your favorite wood cutting board and arrange the ingredients as a pre-dinner nosh.

NOTES: *The prep time of 10 minutes may seem misleading, because of course it's based on you having already done all the work of preparing the delicious appetizers listed. That said, pulling together this platter doesn't have to require days of work ahead of time: some of the items can be made up to a month ahead and pulled out of the freezer or fridge when needed.*

How many people this platter will serve depends on whether you're using a full batch of each recipe. If you're serving full batches, this could easily serve upwards of 18 or 20 people—enough for a party. In that case, I suggest you make two or even three batches of the crackers and chips (plantain and/or chicken skin).

"LIFE IS UNCERTAIN.
EAT DESSERT FIRST."

-ERNESTINE ULMER

CHAPTER 9

DESSERT IS IN MY BLOOD

CHOCOLATE HAZELNUT PECAN COLLAGEN BALLS

YIELD: **12 balls**   PREP TIME: **10 minutes, plus 30 minutes to chill**

If you're breathing a sigh of relief at how "normal" this dessert seems, I'm sure you're not alone (but also turn to page 188 for the Blood Orange Chocolate Pots de Crème; there's plenty of adventure still to be had!). Still, if you'll allow me to get literal with you for a minute: yes, collagen is a protein and an important building block in the growth of our hair, skin, nails, and digestive system; and true, it's tasteless and healthy and super easy to add to your daily routine. But have you ever thought about exactly what collagen is? Well, buckle up: beef collagen comes from the hide of a cow; marine collagen is made from fish scales. In summary, that healthy, innocuous white powder you're putting in your coffee and smoothie every day is essentially powdered cow.

If I've grossed you out, well, you knew what you were getting into when you bought this book! Jokes aside, what I'm trying to show you is that once we get past our own arbitrary ideas of what is acceptable or unacceptable when it comes to eating animals, we can explore even more nutritious and delicious meals than ever before. So let's get you accustomed to powdered cowhides, shall we?

½ cup raw hazelnuts

½ cup raw pecans

3 tablespoons unflavored grass-fed collagen powder

3 tablespoons chocolate- or vanilla-flavored protein powder

3 tablespoons shredded unsweetened coconut, plus more for rolling if desired

2 tablespoons cacao powder

½ cup smooth pecan butter (unsalted and unsweetened)

2 tablespoons maple syrup

3 tablespoons full-fat coconut milk or filtered water, plus more as needed

1 teaspoon vanilla extract

¼ teaspoon ground cinnamon

Pulse the nuts in a food processor until they're finely crushed but not powdered. (I keep the pieces a little bigger because I like the textural contrast in the final product, but it's up to you!)

Put the crushed nuts in a mixing bowl and add all the other dry ingredients, mixing until incorporated and making sure there are no clumps.

Add the pecan butter, maple syrup, and coconut milk and mix with your hands until a thick dough forms; if it's too dry or crumbly, add a little more liquid. The mixture should stick together.

Form the mixture into 12 balls, about 1 inch in diameter, and place in a glass container so they are not touching each other. If you like, you can roll half of the balls in shredded coconut for added texture and visual interest. Refrigerate for about 30 minutes before enjoying.

NOTES: *This easy recipe can be adjusted to your tastes. Want to switch up the pecans for cashews? Great! Swap the pecan butter for peanut butter, why not? Add chocolate chips—sounds smart to me! You can adjust the sweetness and protein amounts as well. These relatively high-fat, high-protein, collagen-filled treats are dense and quash dessert cravings without being too sweet, and they're great for eating on the go or for kids' snacks. They will keep for at least a week in the fridge or up to 3 weeks in the freezer, but they won't last that long!*

MINT CHOCOLATE COCONUT COLLAGEN CUPS

YIELD: **12 cups**   PREP TIME: **15 minutes, plus 35 minutes to chill**

These treats have everything you need to survive the apocalypse: chocolate (obviously, I don't even have to explain that one); collagen, for the many health benefits it offers; coconut, for satisfying, healthy fat; and mint, because, well, it's refreshing and goes great with dark chocolate. These are like healthier, heartier After Eight chocolates—remember those? They'll impress and delight your friends, and you don't even have to tell anyone how easy they are to make!

⅓ cup coconut manna (a.k.a. coconut butter)

3 tablespoons unflavored grass-fed collagen powder

1 teaspoon peppermint extract

Powdered stevia (optional, for sweetness)

1 cup dark chocolate chips (45% to 60% cacao)

½ teaspoon coconut oil

Coarse sea salt, for topping (optional)

NOTES: *For easy removal, I find that silicone works best—either individual mini muffin cups or a mini silicone muffin pan—but you can also use a metal muffin pan with mini paper liners.*

You don't want to leave these out too long at room temperature, as the coconut oil will make them a little melty. They'll keep for up to 2 weeks in the fridge or up to 2 months in the freezer. Since they taste great cold, they're excellent as a quick and satisfying craving killer straight from the freezer!

Warm the coconut manna in a medium microwave-safe bowl in the microwave for about 20 seconds, until soft enough to stir with a spoon.

Stir in the collagen powder. Add the peppermint extract and stevia to taste, if using, and stir until combined. Set aside.

Put the chocolate chips in a medium microwave-safe bowl and microwave for 30 seconds at a time, stirring between intervals, until almost fully melted. Add the coconut oil and microwave for another 30 seconds, then remove and stir until fully melted and combined.

Carefully spoon about half of the melted chocolate mixture into 12 mini silicone cup molds (or a muffin pan lined with 12 mini paper liners), just enough to cover the bottom. Sprinkle a little coarse sea salt across the tops, if desired, and place in the freezer for 5 minutes.

Remove from the freezer and divide the coconut mixture evenly among the cups, placing about 1 teaspoon in each. Pat the filling down to spread it flat across the chocolate layer in each cup.

Cover the coconut filling with the remaining melted chocolate until fully covered. Garnish with a sprinkle of coarse sea salt, if desired. Place in the fridge until fully set, about 30 minutes.

SWEET CINNAMON CHICHARRONES

YIELD: **6 servings**   PREP TIME: **30 minutes, plus time to refrigerate overnight**   COOK TIME: **1 hour 5 minutes**

Similar to beef jerky (another treat that I love deeply), pork rinds or chicharrones get a bad reputation as an unhealthy choice that only truckers eat at gas stations. Well, I challenge you to find a gas station selling anything this unique and delicious! I haven't tried it yet, but I bet these would taste fantastic crumbled up on top of some high-quality vanilla ice cream—or maybe sprinkled on top of Carnivorchata Bone Broth Ice Cream (page 198).

2 pounds pig skin, cleaned and prepped (see page 176)

Coconut oil spray

¼ cup coconut sugar

Seeds scraped from 1 vanilla bean

1 tablespoon cacao powder, plus more for dusting

1 tablespoon ground cinnamon, plus more for dusting

2 teaspoons coarse sea salt

SPECIAL EQUIPMENT:

Air fryer

NOTE: *These will keep in an airtight container at room temperature for up to 3 days, but ideally you want to consume them right away while they're fresh, hot, and crispy. If you do have leftovers, it's best to throw them back in the air fryer for a few minutes before serving to crisp them up again.*

Pat the pig skin dry. Using a fork, poke holes throughout the skin; this will ensure that it doesn't explode when you fry it!

Spray the skin with coconut oil spray, then rub the surface with the coconut sugar, vanilla bean seeds, cacao powder, cinnamon, and salt.

Using a sharp knife, cut the skin into 1-inch pieces. Preheat an air fryer to 350°F for about 3 minutes, then place the pieces in a single layer, without overlapping, in the air fryer basket and cook for about 5 minutes; watch them carefully so they don't burn. Depending on the size of your fryer, you may have to cook the skin in batches.

Remove the pieces from the fryer and place on a paper towel to cool, blotting any excess fat. Sprinkle more cacao powder and cinnamon on top and serve hot.

BLOOD ORANGE CHOCOLATE POTS DE CRÈME

YIELD: **6 servings**   PREP TIME: **30 minutes, plus 3 hours to chill**   COOK TIME: **5 minutes**

This dessert was inspired by an Italian chocolate pudding that uses blood, called *sanguinaccio,* which is a much sexier way to say chocolate pudding with blood in it. *Pot de crème* is just a sophisticated French way of saying "bowl of cream," and that's really what this dessert is: the cream and blood create a soft, puddinglike texture, while the addition of gelatin turns it into something a little closer to a set custard. Either way, it's delicious! I added blood orange to this recipe because, well, I like to be consistent, and blood orange is a gorgeous and fun way to switch up your citrus. It doesn't taste much different from a typical orange—perhaps a bit less sweet, with a grapefruit-like tartness at the end, but it works perfectly in this recipe. The end result is a more hardcore and nutritious version of those chocolate oranges you might get at Christmastime.

¼ cup filtered water

1 tablespoon unflavored grass-fed gelatin

1 vanilla bean

¾ cup whole milk

¾ cup heavy cream

½ cup pork blood

½ cup coconut sugar

1 cinnamon stick

1 teaspoon espresso powder (optional, for a richer, deeper flavor)

¼ teaspoon ground cardamom

¼ teaspoon coarse sea salt

6 ounces dark chocolate (75% cacao or higher), chopped

Grated zest and juice of 1 blood orange

FOR GARNISH:

Finishing salt of choice

Grated zest of 1 blood orange, or 6 blood orange slices

In a large bowl, combine the water and gelatin, then set aside to bloom for 5 minutes.

Scrape out the vanilla seeds from the pod; set aside.

In a small saucepan over medium heat, combine the milk, cream, blood, sugar, cinnamon stick, espresso powder (if using), cardamom, and salt. Simmer, stirring continually with a wooden spoon, until the mixture is fully combined and starts to thicken slightly, about 5 minutes; you'll notice it begin to coat the spoon. (Blood is a natural thickening agent.)

Just when the mixture starts to bubble or steam slightly, stir in the chocolate, blood orange zest, and vanilla seeds until fully incorporated.

Add the gelatin mixture and stir until fully incorporated; it will look darker and thicker but still smooth. Remove the pan from the heat and let cool for 15 minutes. Discard the cinnamon stick.

NOTES: *You can make this dessert without blood, of course, but where's the fun in that? That's just chocolate pudding, and anyone can do that. The addition of blood imparts a richer, deeper flavor (but you won't taste the blood at all; this is a crowd-pleasing chocolate dessert through and through). If you're able to source fresh blood, it really isn't that scary to work with; it's mild smelling and incorporates really well into the recipe, imparting a beautiful color, flavor, and dose of iron and minerals that, when combined with high-quality dark chocolate, basically means you can also call this dessert a superfood! This thick, creamy delight will keep in an airtight glass container in the fridge for up to a week.*

Transfer the pudding mixture to the bowl in which the gelatin bloomed and blend with an immersion blender on medium speed until the gelatin is fully mixed in and the texture is thick, about 5 minutes; add the blood orange juice in the last 30 seconds of mixing. At this point, the mixture should be a deep brown color and have a thick puddinglike consistency.

Cover and chill the pudding in the fridge for 3 hours, until fully cool. It will develop a slightly thicker, denser consistency.

To serve, scoop the pudding into six 7-ounce serving bowls. Sprinkle salt on top, garnish with the grated blood orange zest or blood orange slices, and serve.

MAPLE BACON CHOCOLATE CHIP COOKIES

YIELD: **12 cookies**   PREP TIME: **10 minutes**   COOK TIME: **20 minutes**

Chocolate chip cookies are never a bad idea; this is just a fact. Adding bacon to anything is also never a bad idea, and since any good cookie requires a bit of fat, the addition of bacon fat to this recipe is basically the result of the most delicious science experiment ever. Bacon fat adds a smoky depth that keeps these cookies from being overly sweet; they actually make a good breakfast on the go for the chocolate or bacon lover in your life, and doesn't everyone fall into at least one of those categories? For the maple syrup, I prefer Grade B or dark amber for a deeper, stronger flavor. Ultimately, chocolate chip cookies are a staple of happiness in every household, and this is just a slightly different take on an enduring classic.

4 slices bacon

1 cup blanched almond flour

¼ cup unflavored grass-fed collagen powder

Pinch of coarse sea salt

2 tablespoons bacon fat (room temperature)

2 large eggs

3 tablespoons maple syrup

1 teaspoon vanilla extract

½ cup mini dark chocolate chips (45% to 60% cacao)

Preheat the oven to 350°F. Line a baking sheet with parchment paper.

Cook the bacon in a skillet over medium heat until it is slightly crispy (not too chewy, not burned); you want the bacon pieces in the cookies to be crispy.

While the bacon cooks, combine the dry ingredients in a medium bowl.

When the bacon is done, remove it from the skillet and set aside to cool; drain off the bacon fat and save it for another use. (For this recipe, you want the fat to be at room temperature so that it has a solid, not liquid, consistency.) Once the bacon is cool, crumble it into bacon bit–sized pieces.

Add the crumbled bacon and bacon fat to the dry mixture and combine the ingredients well with your hands, making sure the bacon and fat don't clump.

Add the eggs, maple syrup, and vanilla and combine with your hands until you have a slightly sticky dough. Fold in the chocolate chips.

Scoop up 1 heaping tablespoon of the dough and place it on the lined baking sheet; form the dough into a neat disc shape with wet hands. Repeat with the rest of the dough, making a total of 12 cookies and spacing them about 2 inches apart on the baking sheet.

Bake for 10 minutes, until the edges are a little golden and the centers are firm; if you stick a toothpick into the middle of a cookie and it comes out clean, they're done!

MACA MARSHMALLOWS

YIELD: about eighteen 1-inch pieces   **PREP TIME:** 15 minutes, plus 3 hours to set   **COOK TIME:** 15 minutes

Gelatin and maca and cacao? Let's talk about this antioxidant-rich treat that will make your skin look good—from the collagen in the gelatin and from the smiling that you will be doing after eating these soft, pillowy treats. Feel free to toss them in some s'mores or hot chocolate or just eat them on their own, like I always do.

Maca: people seem to love it or hate it because it tastes a bit like cacao and dirt had a baby, but I'm into it. It has a subtle nutty, chocolatey sweetness that adds depth to desserts without heavily flavoring them. Maca is a root found in Peru, and it's used frequently in baking, smoothies, and soups, sometimes in its original root form but more commonly in a powdered version. It's long been known across many cultures to boost energy and fertility. Small studies have shown promising results with regular use of maca to improve sexual performance, sex drive, and overall mood, with one study showing improved sperm count and quality in men.

Maca is also nutrient-rich, with 1 ounce containing more than the recommended daily intake of vitamin C, as well as significant amounts of iron, copper, B6, potassium, phosphorous, manganese, and riboflavin. Some studies show that maca may have the power to boost antioxidants in the body, helping protect against cell damage caused by free radicals.

I am all for little changes that can have a big impact. If you're going to eat some tasty marshmallows, why not make them at home with the best possible ingredients? Why not sprinkle in some atypical superfoods that promote health and add a little spice and intrigue to your traditional treats?

1 cup filtered water, divided

3 tablespoons unflavored grass-fed gelatin

4 tablespoons cacao powder, divided

1 cup honey, preferably raw

1 tablespoon maca powder

1 teaspoon vanilla extract

SPECIAL EQUIPMENT:

Candy thermometer

In a medium mixing bowl, combine ½ cup of the water and the gelatin, then set aside to bloom for 5 minutes.

Line an 8-inch square baking pan with parchment paper and sprinkle 1 tablespoon of the cacao powder evenly across the bottom.

In a small saucepan, bring the remaining ½ cup of water and the honey to a low boil over medium-high heat. Boil for about 15 minutes, until a candy thermometer reads 240°F, then remove the pan from the heat. It will bubble steadily but shouldn't boil over, so keep an eye on it!

With a hand mixer running on low speed, slowly and carefully pour the hot honey mixture into the bowl with the gelatin. (Make sure to pour it in slowly and away from the mixer so you don't spray hot liquid sugar all over the place!)

NOTE: *You can make your mallows whatever flavor you want—add some mint extract or cover them in cinnamon sugar— but I like the idea of combining the mildly earthy sweetness of cacao and maca. If you have a stand mixer, it's a great choice for this recipe. It will make steps 4 and 5 go more quickly and effortlessly.*

The marshmallows will keep well in an airtight container at room temperature for up to 2 weeks.

Once incorporated, increase the mixer speed to medium-high and continue to beat until the mixture changes in color from caramel to white, becomes creamy, and increases in volume, 7 to 10 minutes.

When the mixture is fluffy and thick, add the maca, 1 tablespoon of the cacao powder, and the vanilla and continue to mix for about a minute. This will cause it to deflate slightly and make it thicker.

Pour the mixture into the prepared pan and smooth the top with a silicone spatula. (Move quickly if you want smooth-looking marshmallows; the mixture will start to set right away!) Allow to cool and firm up for about 3 hours.

When you're ready to cut and serve, evenly dust the top with the remaining tablespoon of cacao powder. Using a lightly greased sharp knife, cut the marshmallow into 1-inch cubes. Once cut, toss them in more cacao powder so they won't stick together (and they'll look pretty!).

COCONUT CREAM LEMON PUDDING

YIELD: **4 servings**   PREP TIME: **5 minutes, plus 1 hour 15 minutes to set**   COOK TIME: **5 minutes**

It's good to have a lemon dessert recipe handy, because not everything can be chocolate, right? I love incorporating citrus into sweet treats, and this dessert is creamy and refreshing with a really bright lemony flavor thanks to the zest. It is not too rich and is pretty darn healthy, thanks to the fatty coconut cream and grass-fed gelatin. You can top it with whipped cream or berries, layer it with some crumbled Sweet Paleo Crackers (page 212) in a glass serving bowl to create a trifle or parfait, or just enjoy it as-is. There's no reason this couldn't double as a breakfast bowl due to its low sugar and high fat content.

½ cup fresh lemon juice

¼ cup filtered water

2½ teaspoons unflavored grass-fed gelatin

1 (15-ounce) can coconut cream

Grated zest of 2 lemons, plus more for garnish

2 tablespoons honey, preferably raw

⅛ teaspoon fine sea salt

4 lemon slices, for garnish

NOTE: *This pudding will keep in the fridge for up to a week.*

Put the lemon juice and water in a medium bowl. Sprinkle the gelatin over the top and set aside to bloom for 5 minutes.

Whisk the coconut cream and lemon zest in a small saucepan over medium heat until steaming but not boiling, about 5 minutes.

Remove from the heat and pour the steaming cream mixture over the gelatin mixture. Add the honey and salt and whisk until smooth.

Allow to cool for 15 minutes, then cover and refrigerate for at least 1 hour, until set.

Remove the bowl from the fridge. If you prefer a slightly denser, more panna cotta–like texture, leave the pudding as is. Otherwise, using a hand mixer on medium-high speed, whip the pudding until fluffy and smooth, up to 5 minutes. Garnish with lemon zest and lemon slices before serving.

WHITE CHOCOLATE MATCHA COLLAGEN BROWNIE CAKE

YIELD: **8 servings**   PREP TIME: **10 minutes, plus 1 hour 15 minutes to chill**   COOK TIME: **20 minutes**

I originally intended this to be a more traditional cake with a light texture, but it ended up dense and fudgy, and I went with it. I know a lot of chocolate purists who don't like white chocolate—perhaps because it is very sweet and usually doesn't have much cacao in it—but I'm an equal-opportunity chocolate lover, and in this recipe, the sweet creaminess of white chocolate evens out the earthiness of the powdered green tea for a surprisingly complex flavor. The crispy caramelized edges of this cake are especially tasty! If you must, dark chocolate works really well here, too.

4 ounces white baking chocolate, chopped

¼ cup coconut oil, plus more for the pan

1 cup coconut sugar

3 tablespoons matcha powder, plus more for garnish

2 tablespoons unflavored grass-fed collagen powder

2 tablespoons vanilla-flavored protein powder

3 large eggs

White chocolate shavings, for garnish (see Notes)

NOTES: *To make white chocolate shavings, I run a block of baking chocolate across my stainless-steel cheese grater.*

This addictive treat is best served chilled. It will keep for up to a week in the fridge.

Preheat the oven to 375°F and grease a 9-inch round cake pan with coconut oil.

Heat the white chocolate and coconut oil in a small microwave-safe bowl in the microwave in 30-second intervals, stirring between intervals, until melted and completely smooth.

In a large bowl, combine the melted white chocolate mixture with the dry ingredients using a wooden spoon.

Add the eggs and whisk until completely smooth.

Pour the batter into the greased pan. Bake until the center looks firm and a toothpick inserted in the middle comes out clean, about 20 minutes.

Allow the cake to cool for 15 minutes, then place in the fridge to cool completely, at least 1 hour.

Cut the cake into 10 slices, dust with matcha powder, top with extra chocolate shavings for additional prettiness and earthiness, and serve.

CARNIVORCHATA BONE BROTH ICE CREAM

YIELD: **4 servings**   PREP TIME: **5 minutes, plus 1 hour to set**

Let's call this what it is: an excuse to eat ice cream—not that you need one. It's also a great way to sneak in the health benefits of bone broth without having to taste it or even tell anyone—your dinner guests or kids will have no idea that their rich, decadent ice cream is full of health-promoting collagen and fatty acids. This super simple but crowd-pleasing recipe, which tastes a lot like an ice cream version of that delicious, creamy, cinnamon-y Mexican drink horchata, is a great reminder that it's surprisingly easy to make healthier versions of treats you love without sacrificing flavor or fun.

You may notice the presence of two ingredients that aren't typical in ice cream: flour and baking soda. Both serve to enhance the texture of this treat: the flour adds to the creamy thickness while the baking soda gives it some airiness so it's not too dense. This isn't exactly a diet food, but at least you can control the ingredients that are going into your desserts. You can change the flavor, of course, if you're not a maple cinnamon person—dark chocolate would be another great option, and you could throw in some fresh berries, chocolate chips, or nuts for texture.

1 (13.5-ounce) can full-fat coconut milk

½ cup chicken bone broth (page 52)

⅓ cup maple syrup

⅓ cup blanched coconut flour

¼ cup unflavored grass-fed collagen powder

1 teaspoon cacao powder (optional)

1 teaspoon ground cinnamon

¼ teaspoon ground nutmeg

¼ teaspoon baking soda

NOTE: *The ice cream should keep for up to 2 weeks in the freezer, but I doubt it'll last that long!*

Put all the ingredients in a blender or food processor and blend for about 3 minutes, until fully mixed and smooth.

Pour the mixture into a freezer-safe glass container and place in the freezer to set for at least 1 hour.

Once frozen, allow the ice cream to soften for about 5 minutes at room temperature before adding the toppings of your choice and serving.

TART CHERRY BEDTIME GUMMIES

YIELD: **12 to 16 gummies**   PREP TIME: **5 minutes, plus 1 hour to set**   COOK TIME: **10 minutes**

You're probably already aware of gelatin's healthful properties (if not, read up on them on page 33), but you may not know that tart cherry juice is reputed to have some great properties, too. There are studies showing a mild beneficial impact on sleep quality with the use of tart cherry juice, which is rich in melatonin, a hormone that helps regulate our sleep cycle and prepare our bodies for rest; I also happen to love the deep, tart flavor. If you're going to have a little sweet, chewy treat before bed, you might as well have one that could help you sleep better! Since these are tasty and can be made in all kinds of fun shapes, they're great for kids too; you can trick them into thinking they're eating candy, which isn't as bad as me tricking my friends into eating liver, but amounts to the same thing—helping people make better choices whether they're aware of it or not!

¾ cup tart cherry juice

¼ cup fresh lime juice

3 tablespoons maple syrup or honey

2 tablespoons unflavored grass-fed gelatin

SPECIAL EQUIPMENT:

Silicone gummy molds with at least 12 cavities

NOTE: *These gummies will keep for up to a week in an airtight container at room temperature; once set, the gummies will retain their shape and texture.*

Heat the cherry and lime juices in a small saucepan over medium heat until hot but not boiling. Reduce the heat to low and whisk in the maple syrup until combined.

Slowly add the gelatin 1 tablespoon at a time, whisking until fully dissolved.

Remove the pan from the heat and carefully pour the liquid into the silicone gummy molds. Refrigerate until firm, about 1 hour.

ICED MINTY MOCHA COLLAGEN COFFEE

YIELD: **1 serving**   PREP TIME: **5 minutes**

Coffee, check. Cacao, check. Coconut, check. Collagen, check. We have the four Cs, and we have a delicious health-promoting beverage! Caffeine, when used in moderation as a tool instead of a crutch to get you through the day, can be an excellent nootropic and is full of antioxidants. Cacao is also full of antioxidants and tastes divine. Coconut milk offers a creamy, decadent consistency with plenty of healthy, filling fats. Collagen, as you already know if you've made it this far into the book, is a fantastic source of protein and essential amino acids that improve the health of your gut, skin, hair, and nails. This recipe is so quick and simple, and it really elevates your morning coffee to something that's a treat without guilt or sugar crashes. If you'd like to be a rebel and enjoy this as a hot drink, simply use freshly brewed coffee, warm the coconut milk in the microwave for about twenty seconds or on the stovetop for about three minutes, and, of course, omit the ice cubes.

10 ounces brewed organic coffee, cold

¼ cup full-fat coconut milk or other milk of choice

2 tablespoons unflavored grass-fed collagen powder

1 teaspoon cacao powder

3 or 4 drops mint extract, or to taste

Pinch of ground cinnamon

Stevia, to taste (optional)

Ice cubes, for serving

NOTE: *If you want to make an iced frappuccino-style beverage, make this recipe in a blender: add a few ice cubes to the blender in the second step and blend.*

Pour the coffee into a 20-ounce or larger mug that's wide enough to fit an immersion blender or a handheld milk frother. (A wide-mouth 24-ounce mason jar is ideal.) Make sure you have about 6 inches of headroom at the top.

Add the rest of the ingredients, except the ice, and mix with an immersion blender or milk frother for 1 minute, or until creamy and fully combined.

Add ice cubes and a reusable straw and enjoy!

" VEGETABLES ARE INTERESTING BUT LACK A SENSE OF PURPOSE WHEN **UNACCOMPANIED** BY A GOOD CUT OF **MEAT.** "

-FRAN LEBOWITZ

CHAPTER 10

AWFULLY GOOD SIDES, SNACKS, AND SAUCES

PALEO BEAUTY BREAD

YIELD: **12 slices**   PREP TIME: **5 minutes**   COOK TIME: **35 minutes**

I call this beauty bread because it just sounds nice and because, with the exclusion of gluten (a known inflammatory protein for many people) and the inclusion of collagen (an amino acid that supports the growth of collagen in your hair, skin, and nails), this delicious Paleo-friendly bread can help boost your beauty from the inside out. We know that no amount of moisturizer or makeup will, well, make up for a poor diet. The surefire way to look your best is to take care of yourself and eat well. But sometimes you just want a chewy, tasty piece of bread, and I won't begrudge you that! This is as simple to make as a typical quick bread and has a nice nutty flavor from the combination of almond flour and flax meal. It holds up well to butter and honey or to savory spreads like Whipped Bone Marrow Butter (page 68), Chicken Liver Mousse (page 126), or Bourbon Bacon Jam (page 216).

1 cup blanched almond flour

½ cup flax meal

¼ cup unflavored grass-fed collagen powder

2 teaspoons baking powder

½ teaspoon fine sea salt

⅓ cup ghee

¼ cup filtered water

2 large eggs

2 tablespoons maple syrup

1 teaspoon apple cider vinegar

NOTE: *This bread will keep for up to 10 days in the fridge or up to a month in the freezer.*

Preheat the oven to 350°F. Line an 8½ by 4½-inch loaf pan with parchment paper, leaving an inch or two hanging over the sides of the pan for easy removal of the bread later.

Put all the ingredients in a blender or food processor and pulse until combined and smooth.

Pour the batter into the lined loaf pan. Bake for 35 minutes, or the bread is until golden on top and a toothpick inserted in the middle comes out clean. Remove from the oven and let cool and set up for 20 minutes, then remove from the pan, slice, and serve.

BLUEBERRY BANNOCK

YIELD: **6 servings**　PREP TIME: **5 minutes**　COOK TIME: **15 minutes**

This recipe is an homage to classic Canadian culture, cuisine, and ingredients. Bannock is a traditional food of the First Nations people. Also called a "quick bread," it's a fun snack for many camping Canadians since it's historically made over a fire; you just wrap the dough buns in foil and throw them in the fire for a few minutes. Bannock is truly a simple pleasure, made easily and quickly with only a few ingredients, and the taste is pure comfort: not overly sweet or dense, like a light scone. I decided to add blueberries since that's the fruit of my native land, Nova Scotia. (This maritime province is the wild blueberry capital of Canada and our largest fruit crop; and blueberries happen to be one of the lowest-sugar, highest-nutrient fruits on the planet.) Who knew that gluten-free bread could be so easy and so delicious, and that you don't need a ton of extra ingredients, sugars, and preservatives to create something amazing? Make a batch of these alongside the Tongue Hash with Peppers, Onions, and Potatoes (page 80) for a hearty brunch! Or top them with Bourbon Bacon Jam (page 216) for the ultimate savory-sweet combination.

½ cup blanched almond flour

½ cup coconut flour

½ cup coconut sugar, plus more for sprinkling

2 tablespoons baking powder

½ teaspoon fine sea salt

½ teaspoon ground cardamom

½ teaspoon ground cinnamon

1½ cups filtered water

½ cup coconut oil, softened

½ cup blueberries

FOR SERVING:

Butter, honey, extra coconut sugar, and/or extra berries

Preheat the oven to 350°F. Line a baking sheet with parchment paper.

Mix all the dry ingredients in a large bowl.

Add the water, coconut oil, and blueberries. Mix well with wet hands; the dough should be sticky and thick, not runny. If the dough is too thin, sprinkle in a bit more almond flour as needed.

Divide the dough into 6 equal pieces, then roll each piece into a ball with your hands and flatten to about 1 inch thick. Place on the lined baking sheet.

Bake for 15 minutes, or until a toothpick inserted into the middle of a bannock comes out clean. Remove from the oven and let cool for about 10 minutes.

Top with more berries, coconut sugar, butter, or honey, if desired, and serve warm.

NOTE: *You can add any berries or other add-ins you like or make it savory by omitting the coconut sugar and sweet spices and adding herbs or cheese and replacing the coconut oil with ghee or lard. These will keep for up to 10 days in an airtight container at room temperature or in the fridge or up to 2 weeks in the freezer.*

SEA SALT PALEO CRACKERS

YIELD: **6 servings**   PREP TIME: **5 minutes**   COOK TIME: **10 minutes**

You can dress up these simple crispy crackers any way you like: add different dried herbs or seeds (like sesame or finely chopped pumpkin seeds) and/or top them with grated cheese. They are a super healthy and surprisingly simple alternative to typical grocery store crackers and go well on a charcuterie plate (see page 178). They also go great with the chopped liver on page 128.

1 cup blanched almond flour

¼ cup coconut flour, plus more for rolling

½ teaspoon fine sea salt

½ teaspoon ground black pepper, plus more for finishing if desired

1 tablespoon dried rosemary leaves, plus more for finishing if desired

2 tablespoons unflavored grass-fed collagen powder (optional, for extra protein)

3 tablespoons extra-virgin olive oil

2 large eggs

Coarse sea salt, for finishing (optional)

NOTE: *These crackers will keep for up to a week in an airtight container at room temperature.*

Have 2 oven racks in the oven, spaced equidistantly. Preheat the oven to 450°F.

In a large bowl, stir together all the dry ingredients.

In a small bowl, whisk together the olive oil and eggs.

Slowly add the wet ingredients to the dry, using wet hands to mix them together. The dough may be a little sticky, and that's okay; just make sure it's mixed well and not clumpy. Divide the dough into 2 equal portions.

Generously sprinkle coconut flour across a large piece of parchment paper; place one of the pieces of dough on the parchment and sprinkle more flour over the dough to prevent sticking. Place another large piece of parchment paper on top and roll out the dough until it's *very* thin, about 1/16 inch (think cracker thin!).

Remove the top piece of parchment paper. Using a pizza cutter, cut the dough into crackers of your desired shape and size, but don't separate them; they'll break apart easily after baking. Sprinkle the dough generously with coarse sea salt and more rosemary and/or black pepper, if desired.

Transfer the bottom layer of parchment paper with the crackers onto a baking sheet. Repeat with the second portion of dough, using a second baking sheet.

Place both pans in the oven and bake until the crackers just turn golden brown, about 10 minutes. They burn quickly, so watch them closely!

Let the crackers cool completely on the pans, about 10 minutes, before breaking apart and serving.

SWEET PALEO CRACKERS

YIELD: **6 servings**   PREP TIME: **10 minutes**   COOK TIME: **5 minutes**

These may be a little closer to really thin gingersnaps than crackers, but whatever you call them, they will satisfy your sweet and crunchy cravings. Crumbled and mixed with butter, they would make a great pie crust, be fantastic sprinkled on top of Carnivorchata Bone Broth Ice Cream (page 198), or be a wonderful addition to a trifle or pudding. They're so easy to make and are a great alternative to similar grocery store crackers without any unpleasant hidden ingredients. They go over well as a kids' snack or movie night treat—you can even make mini s'mores with them!

1 cup blanched almond flour

¼ cup coconut flour or gluten-free baking flour blend

¾ cup coconut sugar, plus more for finishing

1 tablespoon ground cinnamon, plus more for finishing

¼ teaspoon ginger powder

¼ teaspoon fine sea salt, plus more for finishing

2 tablespoons unflavored grass-fed collagen powder (optional, for extra protein)

1 large egg white

2 tablespoons coconut oil, melted

NOTE: *I find this cracker dough much less sticky than the dough for the savory crackers on page 210; however, if you find this dough sticky and difficult to work with, you can dust the bottom piece of parchment paper and the top of the dough with flour before rolling it out.*

These crackers will keep for up to a week in an airtight container at room temperature.

Have 2 oven racks in the oven, spaced equidistantly. Preheat the oven to 450°F.

In a large bowl, stir together the flours, coconut sugar, cinnamon, ginger powder, salt, and collagen powder, if using, until well mixed.

Add the egg white and melted coconut oil. Using wet hands, combine the ingredients until the dough becomes sticky and you can pack it into a ball. If it's too dry and doesn't pack together, add a bit of filtered water. You don't want it to be runny!

Divide the dough into 2 equal portions. Place a portion of dough between 2 large pieces of parchment paper and roll out the dough with a rolling pin until it's almost paper thin, about 1⁄16 inch (think cracker thin!).

Remove the top piece of parchment paper. Using a pizza cutter, cut the dough into crackers of your desired shape and size, but don't separate them; they'll break apart easily after baking. Sprinkle more coconut sugar, cinnamon, and salt over the top of the dough.

Transfer the bottom layer of parchment paper with the crackers onto a baking sheet. Repeat with the second portion of dough, using a second baking sheet.

Place both pans in the oven and bake until the crackers just turn golden brown, about 5 minutes. They burn quickly, so watch them closely!

Let the crackers cool on the pans for about 15 minutes before breaking apart and serving.

PLANTAIN CHIPS

YIELD: **4 servings**   PREP TIME: **10 minutes**   COOK TIME: **25 minutes**

You can use any spices you like on your plantain chips, although garlic powder and cayenne are my favorites. Paprika works well, too. You can also make sweet plantain chips: just get very ripe plantains instead of green ones and toss them with coconut oil spray, cinnamon, and coconut sugar. If you don't have an air fryer, you can make these chips in the oven: preheat the oven to 400°F, place the chips in a single layer on a cooling rack set inside a rimmed baking sheet, and bake for about 20 minutes, until they start to brown. I prefer the double-fried air fryer method because it's quicker and the chips get crispier, more like the ones you get in the store. These make great dippers for Chicken Liver Mousse (page 126)!

2 large green plantains

Extra-virgin olive oil cooking spray

¼ teaspoon garlic powder, plus more for finishing if desired

¼ teaspoon ground black pepper, plus more for finishing if desired

¼ teaspoon cayenne pepper (optional), plus more for finishing if desired

¼ teaspoon coarse sea salt, plus more for finishing if desired

SPECIAL EQUIPMENT (recommended):

Air fryer

NOTE: *In my experience, these chips don't keep very well; even when stored in an airtight container, they may become a little stale and lose their crunch overnight. If you must hold on to them for a day or two, toss them back in the air fryer for a few minutes before serving.*

Using a sharp knife or a mandoline, slice the plantains thinly (about ⅛ inch thick) on an angle to maximize the surface area.

Put the plantain slices in a bowl. Spray liberally with olive oil spray; add the spices and salt and toss with your hands until the chips are well coated.

Lay the plantain slices in a single layer in the air fryer basket. You will need to work in 2 batches.

Turn the air fryer to 375°F and bake for 5 to 7 minutes, checking halfway through to toss the chips and make sure they aren't burning. Just as they begin to look dry and brown, place the chips in a medium bowl lined with a paper towel; then air-fry the next batch.

When all the chips are done, let them cool in the bowl for 5 minutes before tossing them all back into the air fryer for another 5 minutes to ensure they are all extra crispy without burning.

Remove from the air fryer, put the chips in a medium heat-safe bowl, toss with a little extra salt and/or spices, if desired, and serve hot.

BOURBON BACON JAM

YIELD: **about 1 cup (8 servings)**   PREP TIME: **5 minutes**   COOK TIME: **4 hours 10 minutes**

The recipe for this incredible spread was contributed by this book's photographer—and one of my best friends—Heather MacDonald. She is known for creating decadent and sometimes complex meals that delight and wow her friends, but here we are keeping things simple. According to Heather, this jam is perfect on toast with a sunny-side-up egg but works just as well on crusty bread or crackers, because we all know you can't go wrong with bacon. I know from experience that it's the perfect mix of salty, fatty, and sweet, and frankly, it's tough not to just eat it out of the jar with a spoon!

2 pounds regular-cut bacon

5 cloves garlic

1 yellow onion

½ cup bourbon

¼ cup coconut sugar

¼ cup maple syrup

2 tablespoons ground cumin

1 teaspoon crushed mustard seeds

1 teaspoon ground black pepper

1 bay leaf

NOTE: *This jam will keep for up to 2 weeks in the fridge.*

Cut the bacon into strips about the size of your thumb.

In a 12-inch cast-iron skillet over medium-high heat, cook the bacon until browned and almost crisp, about 7 minutes.

While the bacon cooks, peel and roughly chop the garlic and onion.

Put the bacon, rendered bacon fat, garlic, onion, bourbon, coconut sugar, maple syrup, cumin, mustard seeds, pepper, and bay leaf in a Dutch oven or 6-quart slow cooker. Cover and cook on low for 4 hours.

Remove the bay leaf and, using an immersion blender or a regular blender, blend until combined but not completely smooth; you want some texture from the bacon.

Transfer the jam to a glass jar and let cool to room temperature before serving, or refrigerate until ready to serve.

AVOCADO AIOLI

YIELD: **about 1 cup (8 servings)**   PREP TIME: **5 minutes**

Not quite guac, not quite aioli, but very delicious and perfect with some salty plantain chips (see page 214). This dip is smooth and creamy without being overly dense or rich, with a zip from the citrus and the perfect amount of garlicky tang. Avocado is one of my major food groups, and while I'd recommend some sliced avocado on the side of nearly every dish in this book, sometimes it's fun to change things up a little. This makes a great dip for Crispy Fried Chicken Livers (page 124) or any of your favorite chips or raw veggies.

1 large ripe avocado, peeled and pitted

⅓ cup mayonnaise

2 cloves garlic, minced

1 tablespoon fresh lime juice

1 tablespoon fresh parsley leaves, finely chopped

½ teaspoon coarse sea salt

¼ teaspoon ground black pepper

¼ teaspoon paprika

NOTE: *Store in the fridge for up to 5 days. The flavor is actually better after about 24 hours!*

Put all the ingredients in a food processor or blender and blend until smooth.

CHIMICHURRI DIPPING SAUCE

YIELD: **about ⅓ cup (3 servings)**   PREP TIME: **7 minutes**

I have yet to find a protein that doesn't taste good with a little chimichurri! Even elk tongue, as shown, benefits from a spoonful of this bright, herbaceous sauce. Depending on how loose or thick you like your sauce, you can adjust the amount of olive oil. This dipping sauce goes especially well with the Grilled Chicken Heart Skewers (page 112), Bodybuilder Plate (page 136), and Easy Grilled Sweetbreads (page 150).

1 cup fresh parsley leaves

3 cloves garlic, peeled

2 tablespoons fresh lemon juice

2 tablespoons red wine vinegar

½ teaspoon ground cumin

¼ teaspoon fine sea salt

¼ teaspoon red pepper flakes

3 tablespoons extra-virgin olive oil

NOTE: Like anything made with fresh herbs, this sauce is best used right away, although it will keep for up to 5 days in the fridge.

Put everything except the olive oil in a food processor or blender. Pulse on low speed until the ingredients are broken down but not completely liquefied.

Keeping the food processor on low speed, slowly add the olive oil until just incorporated.

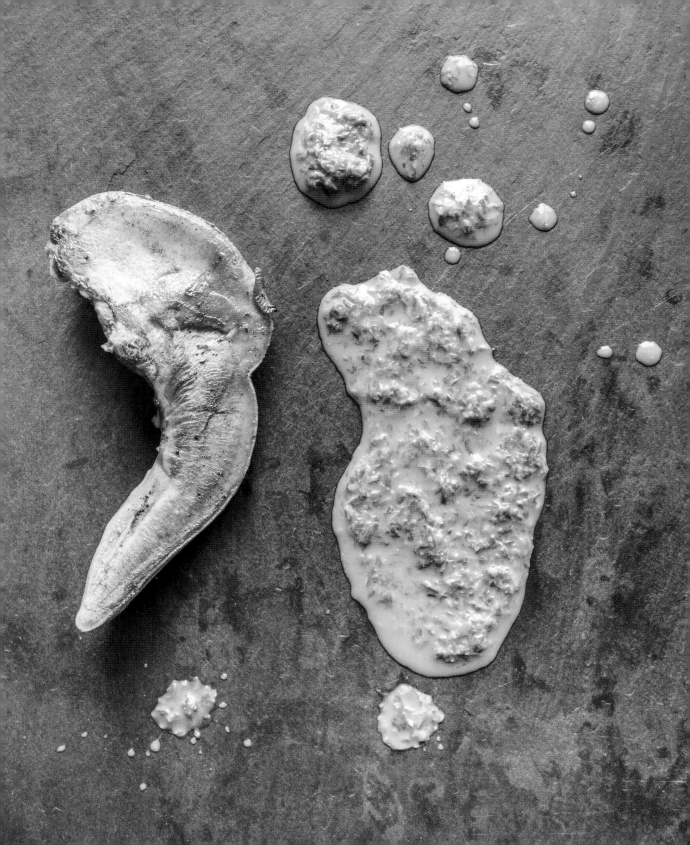

LEMON GARLIC DIPPING SAUCE

YIELD: **about 1 cup (8 servings)**   PREP TIME: **3 minutes**

Rich without being heavy and zippy from the lemon juice and garlic, this sauce goes well with any of the fried dishes in this book. Try it with Crispy Fried Kidney (page 152).

1 cup plain full-fat Greek yogurt

3 tablespoons fresh lemon juice

2 cloves garlic, finely grated

½ teaspoon fine sea salt

½ teaspoon ground black pepper

NOTE: *This sauce will keep for up to 3 days in the fridge.*

Put all the ingredients in a medium bowl and mix until evenly combined. Cover and chill until ready to serve. The sauce can be served straight from the fridge or at room temperature.

THE EASIEST SALAD DRESSING EVER

YIELD: **about 1½ cups (12 servings)**   PREP TIME: **5 minutes**

This dressing plays a starring role in my Cold-Hearted Salad (page 104), but I also use it as a foolproof dressing for a simple green salad to serve alongside many of the offal dishes in this book. This recipe is loosely based on a friend's homemade dressing, but also loosely based on every salad dressing recipe since the beginning of time. Just throw together a little oil, a little acid, a little sweet, and a little salty and mix. Voilà! You can play around with the spices, type of vinegar, or type of mustard to suit your tastes.

1 cup extra-virgin olive oil

¼ cup balsamic vinegar

1½ tablespoons stone-ground mustard

1 tablespoon honey, preferably raw

1 tablespoon fresh lemon juice

½ teaspoon fine sea salt

½ teaspoon ground black pepper

½ teaspoon ground cumin

½ teaspoon paprika (optional)

In a glass container or bowl, stir together all the ingredients until blended, adjusting the acid (the vinegar or lemon juice), oil, and seasonings to taste.

NOTES: *I prefer to use raw honey in all of my recipes, because, since it's not pasteurized, it retains more of its natural healthy antioxidants and nutrients, but regular liquid honey will work here too.*

Keep the dressing in an airtight glass container in the fridge for up to 2 weeks—just shake or mix it up a bit before use.

BALSAMIC BRUSSELS SPROUTS WITH BACON AND ALMONDS

YIELD: **4 servings**   PREP TIME: **5 minutes**   COOK TIME: **15 minutes**

When I was growing up, Brussels sprouts were the poster child for "gross vegetables." I think there was a period in the 1990s when the only way people knew how to eat them was boiled and plain, which of course isn't appealing. I'm glad they've found a new popularity through renewed creativity in preparation, because Brussels sprouts are a tasty, texturally pleasing cruciferous veggie that is, in my opinion, much more versatile than broccoli and tastier than cauliflower. And what is more crowd-pleasing than slightly crispy, caramelized sprouts and bacon, with some almonds thrown in for crunch? I've made this dish many times for family dinners—it's always my contribution to a potluck or Thanksgiving meal. It takes very little finesse and has everyone going back for seconds. This dish would make a great side for the Slow-Roasted Lamb Neck with Rice (page 92) or the Grilled Chicken Heart Skewers (page 112).

2 to 4 tablespoons extra-virgin olive oil

8 ounces bacon, chopped

1 pound raw Brussels sprouts, shredded

2 tablespoons balsamic vinegar

Fine sea salt and ground black pepper

½ cup toasted, unsalted almonds, left whole or chopped

NOTES: *I always purchase preshredded Brussels sprouts, which you can find at most grocery stores. If you're shredding whole sprouts at home, I recommend a food processor—it's much easier than shredding them by hand with a grater!*

This hearty side dish will keep in the fridge for up to 5 days, but it's best eaten fresh when the sprouts are crispy.

Pour 2 tablespoons of olive oil into a 12-inch cast-iron skillet over medium heat. Add the bacon and cook until just beginning to brown, about 5 minutes.

Add the Brussels sprouts and cook until they soften and begin to brown, about 10 minutes, stirring occasionally and adding more oil as needed to keep them from burning.

With about a minute left, stir in the balsamic vinegar; in this last minute of cooking, the sprouts should start to crisp and caramelize.

Season to taste with salt and pepper and scoop the contents of the skillet into a serving bowl. Top with the almonds and serve hot.

KALE WITH SEAWEED AND SESAME

YIELD: **4 servings**   PREP TIME: **5 minutes**   COOK TIME: **9 minutes**

This easy dish has a decidedly Asian feel with the seaweed and sesame seeds and the soy sauce–reminiscent flavor of coconut aminos; it has a light sweetness that would work great alongside some of the grilled recipes in this book, like the Grilled Chicken Heart Skewers on page 112 and the Easy Grilled Sweetbreads on page 150. (You could also throw some grilled chicken hearts on top of this dish and make it a warm salad!) Nori is an edible seaweed or "sea vegetable" that you may recognize as the wrapper for sushi; it has a delicious, crunchy umami flavor when dried and salted that goes great in salads. It's also is a good source of vitamin A, vitamin C, folate, iron, and zinc, among other nutrients. The combination of textures in this recipe, from the soft kale to the nutty toasted sesame seeds and the salty crunch of the seaweed, makes this a more impressive and delightful dish than you'd guess at first glance. Even meat-free dishes can be fun!

2 tablespoons ghee

10 cups destemmed and torn kale

¼ cup coconut aminos

4 sheets dried nori, crumbled

¼ cup toasted sesame seeds (optional)

Coarse sea salt, for finishing

NOTES: *Feel free to experiment with different types of seaweed, like kombu, wakame, and, if you're really adventurous, crushed dulse—they add a ton of vitamins, minerals, and salty flavor to any recipe.*

The sesame seeds are optional, but they go really well with this dish.

This is a dish you really want to eat fresh, as it will wilt and go soggy in the fridge.

Melt the ghee in a 12-inch cast-iron skillet over medium heat.

Add the kale (you may have to add it in batches) and allow to wilt for about 5 minutes.

Add the coconut aminos and toss with a silicone spatula, making sure the kale is coated. Continue cooking for another 3 to 4 minutes, until the kale is completely wilted and some pieces are starting to brown.

Divide the kale among 4 serving plates or bowls. Sprinkle each serving with crumbled nori, toasted sesame seeds (if using), and a little coarse sea salt; serve warm.

DUCK FAT-FRIED POTATOES

YIELD: **4 servings**   PREP TIME: **5 minutes, plus 30 minutes to soak**   COOK TIME: **10 minutes**

I'm going to let you in on a not-very-well-kept secret in the food world: ducks are the most delicious animals to eat. The meat is rich and dark and flavorful, and for some reason the creamy fat has a deep, smoky aroma even when the duck hasn't been smoked. It works really well as a cooking fat, especially in a cast-iron pan. If you ever have the good fortune of cooking duck, save the fat! Use it to cook eggs, put it on roasted vegetables, smear it on bread, and definitely, absolutely fry some potatoes in it. Try these potatoes with the Confit Chicken Gizzards (page 155) or the Offal Omelet (page 168).

1 pound fingerling potatoes

Filtered water

1 teaspoon plus 1 pinch coarse sea salt, divided

2 tablespoons duck fat, plus more as needed

½ teaspoon ground black pepper

½ teaspoon dried rosemary leaves

NOTES: *If you want your fried potatoes extra crispy, throw them in an air fryer for 5 minutes or so after they're done in the skillet.*

These potatoes will keep in the fridge for up to a week—toss them back in the air fryer or a skillet over high heat with a bit more duck fat to reheat and crisp up before serving.

Wash the potatoes and cut off any gnarly bits, but leave the rest of the skin on. Slice the potatoes lengthwise, about ¼ inch thick.

Put the potatoes in a bowl of cold filtered water with a pinch of salt and let sit for 30 minutes; this helps pull the moisture from the potatoes so they get crispier when cooked.

Remove the potatoes from the water and pat dry with a paper towel.

Heat the duck fat in a 12-inch cast-iron skillet over medium heat. Add the potatoes and cook, stirring and adding more fat as needed, until they become crispy on the outside and soft on the inside, about 10 minutes.

Remove from the heat and put the potatoes in a medium bowl. Toss with the remaining 1 teaspoon of salt, the pepper, and rosemary and serve hot.

SUGGESTED MENUS

"
YOU LEARN A LOT
ABOUT **SOMEONE**
WHEN YOU
SHARE A MEAL
TOGETHER. "

-ANTHONY BOURDAIN

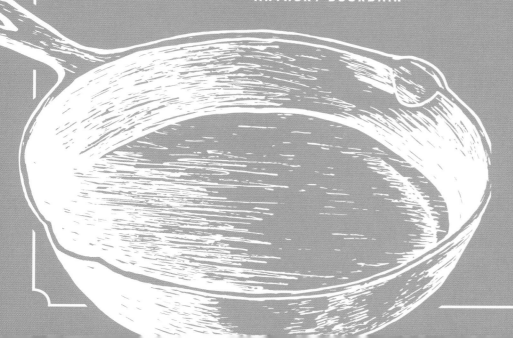

A DAY OF EATING OFFAL FOR BEGINNERS

BREAKFAST

LUNCH

DINNER

DESSERT

Maple Sweet Potato Bone Broth Smoothie Bowl (page 64) with an **Iced Minty Mocha Collagen Coffee** (page 202)

Beefy Baked Meatballs with Chèvre (page 134) and **Lemon Garlic Dipping Sauce** (page 222)

Pork Heart Sausage Sheet Pan Dinner (page 96)

Coconut Cream Lemon Pudding (page 194)

A DAY OF EATING OFFAL FOR ADVENTUROUS EATERS

BREAKFAST

LUNCH

SNACK

Scrambled Brains and Eggs (page 90) with a side of **Savory Blood Pudding** (page 166)

Sliced Beef Tongue Sandwiches (page 78)

Confit Chicken Gizzards (page 155) with **Sea Salt Paleo Crackers** (page 210)

DINNER

DESSERT

Kidney Kebabs with Mint Tabbouleh (page 156) with a side of **Warm Potato Salad with Tripe** (page 158)

Blood Orange Chocolate Pots de Crème (page 188)

FOWL LOVER'S BRUNCH

Savory Oatmeal Breakfast Bowl (page 62)

Chicken Liver Mousse (page 126) and **Chicken Skin Chips** (page 170)

Golden Chicken Bone Broth (page 52)

Foie Gras Profiteroles (page 138)

GAME ON: GAME-DAY SPREAD

 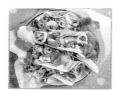  

Greenfield Family Tongue Tacos (page 82)

Grilled Sweetbread Tacos (page 144)

Porky Trail Mix (page 176)

Plantain Chips (page 214) and **Avocado Aioli** (page 218)

Grilled Chicken Heart Skewers (page 112)

Beef Heart Jerky (page 114)

Maple Bacon Chocolate Chip Cookies (page 190)

Chocolate Hazelnut Pecan Collagen Balls (page 182)

CASA QUINTO QUARTO: FAMILY-STYLE DINNER FOR A CROWD

APPETIZER	MAINS	DESSERT

This Charcuterie Plate Is Offal (page 178)

Beefy Baked Meatballs with Chèvre (page 134), **Stuffed Buffalo Heart** (page 116), **Venetian Liver and Onions** (page 122), and **Sautéed Sweetbreads and Fig Salad** (page 148)

White Chocolate Matcha Collagen Brownie Cake (page 196)

PALEO PARTY

Bourbon Bacon Jam (page 216) on **Paleo Beauty Bread** (page 206)

Slow-Cooked Sweet Beef Cheeks with Cardamom and Vanilla (page 84) with a side of **Balsamic Brussels Sprouts with Bacon and Almonds** (page 226)

Carnivorchata Bone Broth Ice Cream (page 198) and **Sweet Cinnamon Chicharrones** (page 186)

LOW-CARB LUNCH

Prosciutto-Wrapped Chicken Livers (page 120)

Bacon Liver Burgers (page 132)

Kale with Seaweed and Sesame (page 228)

Mint Chocolate Coconut Collagen Cups (page 184)

A CONVERSATION WITH A FARMER

" UNDERSTAND, WHEN YOU EAT MEAT, THAT SOMETHING DID DIE. YOU HAVE AN OBLIGATION TO VALUE IT—NOT JUST THE SIRLOIN BUT ALSO ALL THOSE WONDERFUL TOUGH LITTLE BITS. "

-ANTHONY BOURDAIN

Tara Couture is a military veteran, farmsteader, hunter, butcher, and retired registered holistic nutritionist in Ontario, Canada. Farming has always been a part of her life, and at her farm, Slow Down Farmstead, she has dedicated herself to learning and sharing the best practices of caring for animals and providing the best-quality meat. She doesn't shy away from the uncomfortable or gross or sad parts of farming and livestock care; in fact, she celebrates all of it in equal measure as essential components of being alive, human, and part of the food chain. As a result, she's more connected to the animals, the earth, and her own mortality than I believe most of us are. For all these reasons, I was honored to speak with Tara about how her work can help make the world a better place for all of us, plants and animals alike. Here is an excerpt from our chat.

ASHLEIGH VANHOUTEN: Did you always know that you wanted to own, work on, and be part of a farm? Did you grow up in a farming environment?

TARA COUTURE: Yeah. We lived on the corner of my grandparents' farm when I was a little girl in Manitoba. Those memories were always the most profound for me. I would hop the fence and go lick the cow's salt lick and race the bulls to the fence line. I would be there curling up in a tractor tire and playing with stones. Those were the fundamental formations of what I wanted to get back to my entire life.

As you know, Ashleigh, my husband spent twenty-five years in the military, so we moved every two years maybe. I always felt like a bit of a gypsy, and I always wanted to lay roots somewhere, but we just couldn't do that until about ten years ago, when we bought our first farm. Circumstance had to come together with money and where we were in our lives.

We always held that in our hearts. I knew it was going to happen. I meditated on it. I manifested it. I didn't know how it was going to happen, but we set ourselves up and put everything in line. I volunteered on farms everywhere we lived. Every time we got posted to a new place, I would go out and find my farmers, so we had our food. These things were always integral to how we lived.

AVH: You said your first farm was bigger, you had more animals, and you were more focused on providing for the community versus predominantly for yourself. Can you talk about that process? Was it a goal to create a farm that would sustain the community and make you money and then transition into something that was a little more pared-down?

TC: That was always the plan. I mean, I feel very passionate about raising animals humanely. I had an incredible mentor in my life. He was a lifelong cattleman in Alberta. I would squirrel away weeks at a time and go spend time with him. He taught me how to do on-farm slaughter, and he taught me about butchering. He shared with me all about what it was to be connected to the land and the animals. He was just the biggest gift in my life as far as friendship and really learning from someone who was so deeply, deeply connected.

I was so driven to contribute and to be connected and to provide food like that for people from our own land—or the land we were using; I don't really think anyone can own land. We went into farming with my mentor, other friends and farmer friends, and we were always using our free time learning about these things and reading books and going to farming conferences. Before we even had land, we were doing that.

We bought a 200-acre farm, and we were selling grass-fed beef. You have to make a lot of concessions when you're doing things to sell to other people, because it's very expensive to raise animals in the way that I wouldn't compromise on. In Canada, we cannot do on-farm slaughter and legally sell that meat. As you know, we also can't sell raw milk. This stuff happens, but it's very underground. If you get caught, you can lose everything.

There could be a whole book about the cost of setting up water systems, fences, buying your base livestock. It goes on and on and on. Of course, it's not just monetary. You're basically buying yourself a way of living that to us was really important.

We had made the decision that we wanted to downsize and slow down, and we started looking around to see if there was a way we could do that, to have the lifestyle that we wanted, to still be working on the land and contribute, but on a smaller scale.

AVH: The biggest takeaway from that for me is how incredibly complex, difficult, time-consuming, and expensive it is to run a farm that, as you said, has super-high standards. You're constantly working to solve every issue, whether it's pests, irrigation, weather, having enough resources. It's never-ending.

Learning more about your work has given me so much appreciation for the farmers and farms who are willing to do this job for the rest of us so that we can have the health benefits. You have to be so passionate about it, because it's so difficult. And often people who don't know about farming will think, "Of course it's a lot of work; but if this is the natural way of doing things, that's got to make it a little easier, right?" No. Not at all. It's so much work.

TC: It's never-ending. You just have to get into the mindset. There's a lot of humility that goes with looking around and seeing fifty things that need to be done and saying, "Well, it's okay because I did this one thing today." It's a big mind shift, and you have to allow yourself that gift of accepting things that are never quite done, which can be hard for some personalities.

AVH: Absolutely. What does your farm look like now? You said it's mostly self-sustaining, and then you've got a little bit of extra that you use for bartering or selling.

TC: There's quite an underground network of food that moves around farms. For us, we have milking cows and beef cows. We have twelve-head right now of cattle, and that should be eighteen in the spring when they start having babies. That's pretty much maxed out for us. We used to keep a bull, but now we lease a bull from friends of ours, so that was another thing that changed.

We have breeding pigs. We raise heritage pigs on pasture, and they get supplemented with organic feed. All the feed here is organic, which is very important to me. I have some friends and farmers who buy young piglets from us.

We also sell live milking cows. Well, they're called heifers, so a young cow once she's weaned from her mother. When we got into farming, there was a real problem with finding A2 milk [milk without the problematic A1 protein aberration that some people have a hard time digesting]. We had a hard time finding A2 milk cows that could do well on grass alone, because dairy cows are really bred to be dependent on grain.

We went through over thirty animals trying to find the proper genetics of a heritage breed animal that could do well on grass alone, that could raise her calf and could produce A2 milk. That took a really long time. Now, when we have excess young animals, we'll sell them live to other small farms that are looking for those types of genetics in cows. Actually, we have a waiting list!

Then we have ducks, geese, hens, and turkeys. We have meat rabbits. We have a little bit of everything. All of our animals are heritage-breed animals, because they have that vitality. Diversity is really important to us, because every animal plays a different role. Then we sell our excess, what we don't need for our family. We also barter some of our food with other farmers.

AVH: Can you tell us what the difference is between milking and beef cattle—why they're different and how they're different?

TC: Yeah, sure. There are different breeds. Milking cows, you've probably seen them where they almost look skinny, but it's just that they put all their fat into their milk. Normally, the milk that you buy in stores is coming from a Holstein, they're the black and white cows that people are familiar with, and they produce a large volume of milk. They do not have very much butterfat in their milk, and they're typically A1 cows, which has been thought to be causing a lot of the problems with dairy intolerance—not to mention the issues with pasteurization and modernization of milk.

Traditional dairy breeds are Jerseys, Guernseys, and Shorthorns. A lot of them are A2, and you can actually test for that. All of our cows are tested. I've done testing for friends that are farmers as well, to see if their cows are A2. I know a lot of dairies are starting to begin the process of switching to A2-producing cows.

A beef animal will be heavier and fatter. They put on weight a lot differently, they pack on muscle differently. There's a huge variety between those as well. There are these continental breeds, like Sharlee and Limousine, and these type of beef cattle that are huge, but they're big grain gobblers. These are the type of continental breeds that end up in a feedlot system.

Then you have heritage breeds like North Devens, Red Polls, and Herefords, older breeds that have a smaller frame and do really well on grass. Generally, they haven't been bred to get huge on grain like feedlot cattle have.

AVH: I'd love to hear more about your day-to-day work and life. You've got three daughters, and two of them are out of the house now, but they grew up around this and I'm sure were very involved in it. Can you talk about how as a family you run a farm every day?

TC: When our kids were young, we were moving from military base to military base. Like I said, I was always sourcing our food from farmers. We were always spending time at farms. We volunteered on farms. It was really important to me that even though we were in an urban setting, they still had that connection to our food. When it was harvest day, they went and they had to take part in that. Then when we had our own farm, during harvest, they would always take part in that. Every time we would sit down to eat, even before we had our own farm, they would always say, "Who is this animal that we're eating?"

There was a name that went with the animal and a story about where we got it. We always had that connection. To them, that's normal. They couldn't imagine eating something that they didn't know the name of. I know people think that's too intimate and it causes discomfort, but to us it's a beautiful connection and leads to this responsibility. I think we all have to have responsibility for what goes into our mouth, how that animal was raised. I think that's truly caring about the environment and the climate—to have that type of intimate connection to our food.

AVH: I want to go back to one of the things you touched on, the idea of being more intimately acquainted with or aware of the animals you're eating and how uncomfortable that is for people. You say that the uncomfortable part, the butchering and slaughtering and harvesting and all that stuff—no one's pumped about doing that, but it's still important. And if it's uncomfortable, that's fine, because there are aspects of life that maybe should be uncomfortable, because that's going to give you more respect for it and more awareness of the seriousness and intensity of what it means to be alive and to be a part of the life cycle and the food chain. We are so coddled in the Western world; so many of us don't ever expect to have to feel discomfort, or any connection with the work that it takes to nourish ourselves. And for people who eat meat and don't want to know where it came from and don't want to know what it took to get there, that's a privilege we're all allowed to have, but we may not necessarily be benefiting from.

I'd love for you to talk a little more about that. Maybe we can start with your apprenticeship in Alberta with this cattleman. You learned about butchering and stuff through him?

TC: Can I talk about him without crying, that's the question, because he's died.

He was a lifelong cattleman. He was in his sixties when he passed away, but he just got it. He was charismatic and so passionate and loving. When I first started, I asked him to let me come out there and just follow him around. I started doing that every year for quite a few years. I remember the first time I went out there and he had, I think, 7,000 or 8,000 acres of native prairie grasslands. By the way, his son has now taken over the farm, and he's just as brilliant as his father.

He raised bison and beef cattle. These bison were about as close as you would ever get to going back to the time when these animals used to roam and form the soil and were such a huge part of the ecosystem. He had herds of bison that never saw people. You would have to drive for a very long time to find where they were, and they were living how they are supposed to live. There were different groups and different family units.

Anyway, this first time I ever took part in harvesting an animal, we got in the truck and drove for close to forty-five minutes looking for them. I was absolutely terrified. I was like, "What am I doing here? Who am I kidding? What the hell is wrong with me? Why do I keep doing these things to myself?" I thought, "I can't do this. I want to get out of here." Anyway, we found the bison.

He found the animal that he was going to harvest, and he shot the animal from afar. We went to the animal, bled it out. We stayed there, and he spoke to the spirit of the animal. Whether people think that is meaningful or not is irrelevant; it was meaningful to him and it's meaningful to me, so we still do that practice to this day.

It was life-changing for me. I know to some people, it sounds maybe morbid, but it was one of the most beautiful things I had ever experienced. If I can be so indulgent as to explain why: When I was growing up, there was quite a bit of tumultuousness. I was terrified of death, and I was scared that people were going to die and leave and I wouldn't have anyone. It just became consuming; death just seemed so scary to me. I was raised Catholic. I wasn't sure that I'd get to the right place if I died.

If we have faith, we're told to believe something, but the actual experience of death now doesn't reflect that. We don't have wakes at home anymore. You don't have a body sitting in the living room and everyone's talking about old Uncle Joe and what a good guy he was. We hide it and we sanitize it. It's that way with animals too, right? We put it in cellophane and have other people do the work for us.

I just really thought that [the harvest] was going to be violent. I didn't know if I had what it took to take part in that. I thought that it was going to be too much for me, that I was just too compassionate, too sensitive. But something happens when you take part. There's this level of responsibility. That's huge and that has to be felt by people, I think; it can't be explained.

The big thing that happens is that you actually experience the lifting of a soul. I don't want to get too far into that, because some people are probably rolling

their eyes, but you understand immediately that there is a life force there. When that life force is extinguished, that spirit moves on. You experience that, it's tactile. It's real. You can feel that spirit leaving. Suddenly, there is no longer that animal there, but there is meat. That animal goes and leaves you that nourishment.

I've written about this reciprocity that we have: we raise these animals well. We give them the life that they need to be fully realized as the creatures they are, and they nourish the land by grazing it, and they provide nourishment for us when their life is over.

My goal when my youngest daughter moves out is to spend my energy and time in working toward getting farm slaughter legalized in Canada. If people want to buy an animal direct from a farmer that has been harvested in that way, not put in a trailer, not brought into an abattoir [slaughterhouse], but is just on pasture, under the sun, at home, eating grass. It's so instantaneous and humane: a bullet in the brain, and done.

This is legal in some other places. I think that we need to, if we're talking about ethical meat, talk about the ethical and humane slaughter of those animals as well.

[My mentor and I] would spend many hours watching the animals, and he'd say, "You see that one? That one's not finished. That one needs two more months on grass." I'd be like, "What are you looking at?" To me, that one looks like the one beside it. He would say, "No, that one's not finished. That would be a miserable eating experience." He taught me so much.

I could go on about poor grass-finished beef for hours. People are butchering these animals too early, and they're too lean and it's just chewy and there's no fat on it. People say, "Well, that's grass-fed beef." No, it's not. That's improperly finished grass-fed beef. Anyway, that's a different topic.

AVH: Thank you so much for sharing that, because this is intense stuff that we're talking about. I think going back to what you were saying about how harvesting and butchering is the least pleasant part of the work that you do, but it's just as important and deserving of respect as all the work you do caring for the animals before they're harvested and caring for the land. It's something that I think the rest of us privileged people need to hear.

By turning a blind eye to how our meat is slaughtered and prepared and harvested, we are allowing the inhumane feedlot factory farms. We're allowing unpleasant stuff to happen because we aren't willing to look at what the options are, to look at how it could be, to experience what it could be. We're just saying, "We don't want to look at it. We don't want to think about it. Just let me buy my beef in the grocery store and leave it at that." That's what's really allowing a lot of these inhumane practices to continue, right?

TC: Exactly. I've had so many people suggest to me that I'm made of some tough stuff. "Wow, you're strong to be able to do that." It's a hidden insult in a way. If you're compassionate and you really love animals, you could never do that. But I know for a fact they're buying feedlot meat from the grocery store. It's just this cognitive dissonance. And I get it. Our system is set up to buffer that.

But behind that system lies a lot of cruelty and destruction, both for the animals and for our environment, for the land. I really want to pull that back a little bit and to suggest to people that we have to face these things that make us uncomfortable, because that's where growth comes. Who wants to be stagnant in their thoughts and their feelings about things? We need to stretch and be better and do better.

I don't want to be in people's faces with it. Like you said, yes, we need to talk about good practices and everything else, but we also need to carry that through and be really honest about what we're talking about, because creepy things hide in dark shadows. I think that we need to illuminate what's happening. The only way we're going to get better is if we shine a light on what's going on and what's possible. We need to ask questions and demand support for what's possible.

AVH: Absolutely. I don't think there are too many people out there who are like, "I just hate animals across the board," but I don't think there are many people in the world who are caring for animals as much as people like you. I mean, it's one thing to have a pet at home, and it's another to take care of dozens or hundreds of livestock in a loving and healthy and natural way. That's an incredible amount of work. You don't do that if you don't love animals, right? It's just this other way of looking at it that people don't really consider.

TC: Yeah, for sure. The other thing people often assume is that I keep a level of distance from my animals. They'll say, "Oh my God. You put their name on the food package? How do you do that? I could never." I don't think like that. I really feel I have this precious gift of getting to know these animals. Yes, they all have different personalities. It's amazing to give them what they want and watch how they live and learn things from them. I learn things all the time.

I want the full deal. I'm getting this fully realized relationship as much as a cow and a girl can have a relationship. They are not my pets, but I deeply respect them. I find my relationships with them very rewarding. That's what life is, right? I mean, you get to know people, you make friends, you have these relationships with people you love and care about—you hold back from these things and you hold back from life. Yes, that means you're vulnerable to pain, and so what? Pain is life too, and I'd rather give it what I got and have to live with heartbreak than to try and live in a semi-numb state. What's the point of that?

AVH: I feel I'm getting a really good therapy session during this chat, because this is so true. This applies to the rest of life too.

For someone like me who wants to have a bit of this experience and maybe isn't going to go to Alberta and make friends with a cattleman, are there opportunities, without it being voyeuristic, to go and experience a slaughter or spend time on a farm and experience the harvesting process, or any part of it? Or is that something that's closed off from us, even if we want to see it?

TC: It's hard, but it's doable. I think that more people like you should be talking to farmers and expressing an interest in doing it, because the possibility is there. I think more and more people want to somehow participate and be exposed to these things as well. As far as hunting, that's separate, because the best thing to do there is to find a hunter you can go out [on a hunt] with.

I would say ask your farmer if you can be a part of it. Maybe it wouldn't be a beef animal, but it might be pigs, or chickens, or ducks. When we lived on our old farm, we held a course where we did on-farm butchery of two sheep. We just did it outside on these tables, and there were a whole bunch of people there and it was a beautiful, crisp fall day. It was wonderful.

Some people are starting to do on-farm slaughter courses for people, but it's still pretty sporadic. We've thought about opening it up to more people, but it's a little precarious, because who's going to show up? It's a sacred act, and it's very intimate. Our animals know us and everything's calm.

I think this is just stuff that's in the beginning stages; nobody wanted to know before. Probably the best thing is to talk to farmers you're getting your food from and see exactly how you can be involved.

AVH: That makes sense. You mentioned how it's not actually legal in Canada to slaughter animals on-farm for sale. I'm guessing that's a supply chain and regulation issue, like they want it all centralized and done their way instead of allowing individual farms to take care of it themselves. Can you explain that?

TC: In Canada, on-farm slaughter is legal, but you cannot sell or give away that meat. There are states in the US that allow it, and in different parts of the world, it's commonly done. It's a supply chain issue. It's a control issue. They talk about safety. They talk about pathogens. There are so many regulations.

Ultimately, if I was butchering a beef animal here, you, a consumer, [might see] value in the fact that my animal was out on grass and died immediately at home. We're talking no cortisol coursing through its muscle. There are no adrenal glands going haywire because they're under stress of being loaded in a trailer and brought to this abattoir. There's a whole host of issues with that, even when it's done very well. When we have to do that, we handle them the way we always handle them, with care and slowness and patience. I bring them to our local small abattoir, so it's not like a three-hour ride in a semi-trailer with a bunch of other animals. They are handled and offloaded carefully and with patience. Even then, the animals are scared. It's walking into a room that smells like bleach and everything is stainless steel, and there's concrete under its hooves.

And that's the best-case scenario, because it gets a lot worse. Comparing that to what happens if you're able to slaughter an animal right on the pasture, where it's born and has lived its entire life and will die instantaneously and painlessly, it's a very, very different process. And right now, if you saw value in that and were seeking that out as a consumer, I legally could not sell that to you.

AVH: I would imagine that these regulations are probably quite similar in the US, if not even more difficult for small farms to do things the way they want to, because the supply chain and the big guys are even bigger down there.

I wanted to spend some time talking about something that you and I are both passionate about, which is nose-to-tail eating. With that, I mean organ meats— more than just muscle meat. You have a ton of amazing recipes and blog posts and information on your website about this, and I think it's important because we're trying to normalize something [eating all parts of the animal] that actually is normal and has been normal across most cultures and timelines, except for literally just the Western world right now. When you were growing up, were you eating nose-to-tail? Is it something you try to encourage with your community and your family?

TC: Well, first, I did not grow up eating those foods. Okay, that's not totally true. I did grow up eating pâté, because my dad's side of the family is French. Every time I went to my grandma's house, we had pâté. I always loved pâté.

AVH: Delicious.

TC: Yes. Sitting down to a plate of liver or something, no. I got into it because as an adult, our meat was bought in bulk, in the fall after the harvest, after those animals spent the whole summer on pasture. We got whole animals. I was like, "I want everything," and that's what I got. I ended up with all these organ meats and bones and gnarly bits, and I had to figure out a way to make them palatable and enjoyable.

What would I do? Throw them out? Never. It's an important part of eating that animal, not only for the nutrient density, the very exclusive nutrients that you find in these foods, but it's about honoring the animal too.

I started to make my own sausage because our family loves sausage. It's pretty pricey when you're buying high-quality stuff. We would get, let's say, a bison in the fall, and I would take a bunch of ground meat, always with a higher fat percentage, and I would dice up some organ meat into there, like kidneys, and add some spices. I would take it all and press it into a large cookie sheet and then freeze it that way, score it, and break it into little rectangular bars. I would do that in bulk, so I had cheap sausages and were really just ground beef, but with the organ meats mixed in.

Now, when my kids come home to visit, they'll say, "Mom, pick me up with heart tartare." That's their favorite thing. I make heart tartare and pick them up at the train or airport. They get in the car and they're like, "Where's my food?" Because they love it. They grew up eating it.

I still like to experiment with new things. It just becomes part of how you eat. I know if I go a while and I haven't eaten any offal, I start to crave it.

AVH: I'm similar. I didn't grow up eating any offal, and that's the excuse a lot of people tell me when they see the way I eat. They're like, "I didn't grow up eating that way, so I just can't." I'm like, "That's not a thing, guys. Most of us didn't grow up eating that way."

I like to reframe eating nose-to-tail as an exciting thing; it's an opportunity. It's not going to hurt you to try something new, okay? Maybe you have some liver and you don't like it. Fine. You just had an experience. You learned something. You move on.

But maybe you try sweetbreads, or pâté, or heart, or tongue and it's incredible and you have this new, nourishing, exciting world open up to you food-wise and nourishment-wise. It's the idea of keeping your mind open. And what we consider gross and not gross is so arbitrary, right? Even the people who would never want to contemplate where their food came from know on some level that their steak is the flesh of an animal, but the idea of eating organs is just horrific and extreme.

Just think about how arbitrary and ridiculous that is. I'm not trying to make people feel stupid, because we're all going through it at our own pace. But if you think eating one part of the animal is fine and eating another part is crazy, again it's just such a privileged way to approach how we're eating. It's backwards to me.

Okay. People are slowly coming around to this idea—I'm posting about it every day and you're posting about it every day, and I am getting a lot of people who are cautiously interested, right? They're like, "Okay, maybe I can get my head around some chicken liver to start. Maybe I can try to look at some of this stuff." What advice do you have for people who are living in urban environments and are interested in trying out some organ meat?

TC: I get that question a lot. There are a few different things: like you suggested, go see a local butcher. You have to ask what's really going on there, because a lot of local butchers are bringing in commodity or industrialized meat and cutting it up themselves. You still have to question where it's coming from, what the source is, how that animal was fed. If they don't know those things, maybe find a different butcher.

There's also a great website called Eat Wild. It's for both the US and Canada. They have a map, and it'll show farms around you. Then everybody puts up a little blurb about what they're doing, what they're raising, how they're raising it, and what their values are as a farm. It's a resource to contact people and meet the farmers. Any farmer you buy meat or food from should be willing to have you [visit] and show you around and be proud of what they're doing.

Another possibility is the Weston A. Price Foundation, which usually has a chapter in every city.

Spend time in your local farmers markets, and don't be afraid to ask questions. I really think most farmers are working their tails off. I don't recommend people attack them and come across as being pompous and knowing more than they do, because that happens a lot. Just have a respectful conversation. Ask if you could go out and see the farm, if that's possible. Look into CSAs and meat shares.

AVH: If people are interested in organ meat specifically, is there anything different they should be looking for or asking about in terms of safety and quality? I know people have a lot of fear or maybe trepidation around organ meats, because they think they may be inherently more risky or have more chance of carrying parasites or disease or whatever. Is there anything different you should be looking at when you're trying to source organ meats, or is it simply that the freshest, highest-quality animals are going to give you the best product?

TC: For sure, you want to know the sourcing of that animal. I mean, if you consider the amount of antibiotics and topical insecticides and herbicides and then what's in the feed of the conventional animal, I don't want to be eating that liver or kidney, either—I don't want to be eating any part of that animal, to be frank.

Regarding organ meat safety: sometimes I eat raw liver and I don't have a problem with it, but that liver has been frozen for three weeks, which will kill any liver flukes or parasites. I certainly wouldn't go to a grocery store and buy liver and eat that raw. In general, though, inspectors are very over-the-top cautious about inspecting liver and heart. If you ever get a whole organ and see that it's slashed, that's because they're looking inside it for any signs of disease, illness, or parasites. Often, even if you get a heart from a farmer, it'll be cut open for that reason.

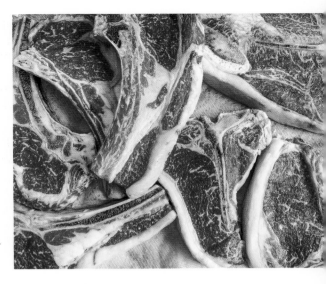

When you buy from a small producer, an inspector is standing there inspecting the entire carcass. If you buy from a big factory meat processor, an inspector might come in once or twice over thousands of carcasses. So that's a huge quality control difference. It's a lot of pressure for the farmer, but for the people eating it, it's way safer to buy from a small farmer because of the demands that we have to meet over food production.

I encourage everyone to eat organically, whether it's meat or organs. But I understand that on a big level it's about economics and it's about food corporations making really cheap food for us and selling it to us as if it's going to save the planet.

AVH: Thank you so much for all of this wisdom. Just to bring things full circle, to the respect that we all should have for our planet, our health, and the animals that sustain us—I don't know if there's a more important topic than to appreciate the life that we're given. It's not about convincing people to eat a certain way or do anything, it's about being grateful for the life and the time that we have. It's about being present in that and all the positive and negative and exciting and scary and happy emotions that come with being alive.

TC: When you drill down the argument, it always comes down to the common denominator that a sentient being had to die for you to eat. My answer is yes, of course it did. This is part of being connected to nature. We're all going to die. Let's stop pretending this is not going to happen by sitting on our couches staring at a TV. Let's start celebrating every day that we have. Death is a part of life, and there is a beauty and reverence in that.

ACKNOWLEDGMENTS

Thank you so much to everyone who helped make this happen:

Alex, my biggest fan: I'm so lucky to have you.

My stepdad: I remember the drives we took when I was a kid, when you asked me what I wanted to be, and instead of saying an astronaut or doctor, I said author. You supported my childhood dreams, and here I am. Thanks for all those midnight barbecued steaks. I miss you every day.

My dear friends Heather and Patty, who shared so much of their time, energy, and creativity in helping me make this book happen, without a second thought. Your talent and generosity are incredible.

My mom, my family and friends, and everyone in my life who will never eat offal, but who supported this project anyway.

And a special thanks to the following people and companies who contributed to this book in various ways:

For offering their insights during interviews with me:
Diana Rodgers, Sustainable Dish
Tara Couture, Slow Down Farmstead

For contributing delicious recipes:
Adam Vettorel, North & Navy
Ben Greenfield and family
Beth Lipton
Cristina Curp, The Castaway Kitchen
Diana Jarrar-Solomon, MAGICdATES
Diane "V" Capaldi, Paleo Boss Lady
Erin Skinner, RD
Joe Heitzberg, Crowd Cow
Nikki DeGidio
Tania Teschke

For contributing ingredients for testing the recipes in this book:
Aurelius Food Co.
BUBS Naturals

RESOURCES

ONLINE PURVEYORS OF OFFAL

Belcampo: belcampo.com

Crowd Cow: crowdcow.com

Force of Nature: forceofnaturemeats.com

U.S. Wellness Meats: grasslandbeef.com

MY FAVORITE INGREDIENT RESOURCES

Bob's Red Mill: bobsredmill.com (for gluten-free, almond, and coconut flours)

Brodo: brodo.com (high-quality premade bone broths)

BUBS Naturals: bubsnaturals.com (the best source of unflavored grass-fed collagen powder for baking)

Fond Bone Broth: fondbonebroth.com (high-quality bone broths you can use in cooking)

Further Food: furtherfood.com (a great place to get grass-fed gelatin powder)

Hu Kitchen: hukitchen.com (delicious Paleo-friendly baking chocolate)

Redmond Real Salt: redmond.life (I love their range of mineral-rich sea salts!)

Udi's: udisglutenfree.com (tasty bread and bun options)

FOR FURTHER READING

Eat Wild: www.eatwild.com

Savory Institute: https://savory.global

Sustainable Dish: sustainabledish.com

Weston A. Price Foundation: www.westonaprice.org

REFERENCES

Brighton, Dr. Jolene. "What Are the Health Benefits of Maca Powder?" Accessed February 24, 2020. https://drbrighten.com/maca-powder-benefits/.

Cosentino, Chris. "The Health Benefits of Consuming Organ Meats." Mercola. December 13, 2013. https://articles.mercola.com/sites/articles/archive/2013/12/30/eating-organ-meats.aspx.

Ethical Omnivore Movement. https://www.ethicalomnivore.org/blog/.

Gonzales, Gustavo F., Amanda Córdova, Karen Vega, Arturo Chung, Arturo Villena, C. Góñez, and Sergio Castillo. "Effect of *Lepidium meyenii* (MACA) on Sexual Desire and Its Absent Relationship with Serum Testosterone Levels in Adult Healthy Men." *First International Journal of Andrology* 34, no. 6 (2002): 367–72.

Kresser, Chris. "How to Eat More Organ Meats." ChrisKresser.com. Accessed January 20, 2020. https://chriskresser.com/how-to-eat-more-organ-meats/.

Mihrshahi, Seema, Ding Ding, Joanne Gale, Margaret Allman-Farinelli, Emily Banks, and Adrian E. Bauman. "Vegetarian Diet and All-Cause Mortality: Evidence from a Large Population-Based Australian Cohort—The 45 and Up Study." *Preventive Medicine* 97 (2017): 1–7.

"Organ Meats: An Evolutionary Perspective." Enviromedica. Accessed February 20, 2020. https://www.enviromedica.com/learn/organ-meats/.

Pigeon, Wilfred R., Michelle Carr, Colin Gorman, and Michael L. Perlis. "Effects of a Tart Cherry Juice Beverage on the Sleep of Older Adults with Insomnia: A Pilot Study." *Journal of Medicinal Food* 13, no. 3 (2010): 579–83.

Rodgers, Diana. "Why I Give a Sh*t About Sustainability." Accessed March 4, 2020. https://robbwolf.com/2017/12/06/why-i-give-a-sht-about-sustainability/.

Sietsema, Robert. "The Offal-Eater's Handbook: Untangling the Myths of Organ Meats." Eater. June 16, 2015. https://www.eater.com/2015/6/16/8786663/offal-organ-meat-handbook-cuts-sweetbreads-tripe-gizzard.

United States Department of Agriculture. "Organic Livestock Requirements." Accessed February 1, 2020. https://www.ams.usda.gov/sites/default/files/media/Organic%20Livestock%20Requirements.pdf.

Wang, Tong, W. R. Teague, Seong C. Park, and Stanley J. Bevers. "GHG Mitigation Potential of Different Grazing Strategies in the United States Southern Great Plains." *Sustainability* 7, no. 10: 13500–21.

"What Are Animal Byproducts?" American Meat Science Association. November 20, 2015. https://meatscience.org/students/meat-judging-program/meat-judging-news/article/2015/11/20/what-are-animal-byproducts.

RECIPE QUICK REFERENCE

RECIPE	PAGE	★	👨‍🍳	30
Golden Chicken Bone Broth	52	✓		
Anti-Inflammatory Turkey Bone Broth	56	✓		
Beef Bone Broth	58	✓		
Bone Broth From The Sea	60			
Savory Oatmeal Breakfast Bowl	62	✓		✓
Maple Sweet Potato Bone Broth Smoothie Bowl	64	✓		✓
Super Sexy Bone Marrow	66	✓		✓
Whipped Bone Marrow Butter	68			
Pork Hock Hodgepodge	70	✓		
Tongue in Tomato Saffron Sauce	74			
Sliced Beef Tongue Sandwiches	78			
Tongue Hash with Peppers, Onions, and Potatoes	80			✓
Greenfield Family Tongue Tacos	82			
Slow-Cooked Sweet Beef Cheeks with Cardamom and Vanilla	84			
Provençal Beef Cheek Daube	86		✓	
Scrambled Brains and Eggs	90		✓	
Slow-Roasted Lamb Neck with Rice	92			
Pork Heart Sausage Sheet Pan Dinner	96	✓		
Deer Dip Sandwiches	100			
Hearty Nightshade-Free Chili	102			
Cold-Hearted Salad	104	✓		✓
Saucy, Spicy Lamb Hearts	106			✓
Paleo Pho	108			
Almond Butter, Raspberry, and Heart Pemmican	110			
Grilled Chicken Heart Skewers	112	✓		
Beef Heart Jerky	114			
Stuffed Buffalo Heart	116			
Prosciutto-Wrapped Chicken Livers	120	✓		
Venetian Liver and Onions	122			
Crispy Fried Chicken Livers	124			
Chicken Liver Mousse	126	✓		
Chopped Liver	128			
Duck Liver Terrine with Blueberry Sauce	129			
Bacon Liver Burgers	132	✓		✓
Beefy Baked Meatballs with Chèvre	134	✓		
Bodybuilder Plate: Mixed Meats with Rice	136			
Foie Gras Profiteroles	138		✓	
Grilled Sweetbread Tacos	144			
Sautéed Sweetbreads and Fig Salad	148			

RECIPE INDEX

IT'S ALL ABOUT THE BONES

 52
Golden Chicken Bone Broth

 56
Anti-Inflammatory Turkey Bone Broth

 58
Beef Bone Broth

 **60**
Bone Broth from the Sea

 62
Savory Oatmeal Breakfast Bowl

 64
Maple Sweet Potato Bone Broth Smoothie Bowl

 66
Super Sexy Bone Marrow

 68
Whipped Bone Marrow Butter

 70
Pork Hock Hodgepodge

FROM THE NECK UP

74
Tongue in Tomato Saffron Sauce

78
Sliced Beef Tongue Sandwiches

80
Tongue Hash with Peppers, Onions, and Potatoes

82
Greenfield Family Tongue Tacos

84
Slow-Cooked Sweet Beef Cheeks with Cardamom and Vanilla

86
Provençal Beef Cheek Daube

90
Scrambled Brains and Eggs

92
Slow-Roasted Lamb Neck with Rice

EAT YOUR HEART OUT

96
Pork Heart Sausage Sheet Pan Dinner

100
Deer Dip Sandwiches

102
Hearty Nightshade-Free Chili

104
Cold-Hearted Salad

106
Saucy, Spicy Lamb Hearts

108
Paleo Pho

110
Almond Butter, Raspberry, and Heart Pemmican

112
Grilled Chicken Heart Skewers

114
Beef Heart Jerky

116
Stuffed Buffalo Heart

LIVER IS THE WURST

120
Prosciutto-Wrapped Chicken Livers

122
Venetian Liver and Onions

124
Crispy Fried Chicken Livers

126
Chicken Liver Mousse

128
Chopped Liver

129
Duck Liver Terrine with Blueberry Sauce

132
Bacon Liver Burgers

134
Beefy Baked Meatballs with Chèvre

136
Bodybuilder Plate: Mixed Meats with Rice

138
Foie Gras Profiteroles

LET'S GET GUTSY

144
Grilled Sweetbread Tacos

148
Sautéed Sweetbreads and Fig Salad

150
Easy Grilled Sweetbreads

152
Crispy Fried Kidney

154
Sautéed Veal Kidneys with Garlic and Onion

155
Confit Chicken Gizzards

156
Kidney Kebabs with Mint Tabbouleh

158
Warm Potato Salad with Tripe

160
Baked Tripe with Zucchini Fries

162
Portuguese Red Wine Tripe Stew

BITS AND PIECES

166
Savory Blood Pudding

168
Offal Omelet

170
Chicken Skin Chips

172
Crispy Salmon Skin Salad

174
Oxtail Stew

176
Porky Trail Mix

178
This Charcuterie Plate Is Offal

DESSERT IS IN MY BLOOD

182
Chocolate Hazelnut Pecan Collagen Balls

184
Mint Chocolate Coconut Collagen Cups

186
Sweet Cinnamon Chicharrones

188
Blood Orange Chocolate Pots de Crème

190
Maple Bacon Chocolate Chip Cookies

192
Maca Marshmallows

194
Coconut Cream Lemon Pudding

196
White Chocolate Matcha Collagen Brownie Cake

198
Carnivorchata Bone Broth Ice Cream

200
Tart Cherry Bedtime Gummies

202
Iced Minty Mocha Collagen Coffee

AWFULLY GOOD SIDES, SNACKS, AND SAUCES

 206
Paleo Beauty
Bread

 208
Blueberry
Bannock

 210
Sea Salt Paleo
Crackers

 212
Sweet Paleo
Crackers

 214
Plantain Chips

 216
Bourbon Bacon
Jam

 218
Avocado Aioli

 220
Chimichurri
Dipping Sauce

 222
Lemon Garlic
Dipping Sauce

 224
The Easiest Salad
Dressing Ever

 226
Balsamic
Brussels Sprouts
with Bacon and
Almonds

 228
Kale with
Seaweed and
Sesame

 230
Duck Fat–Fried
Potatoes

GENERAL INDEX

ABOUT THE AUTHOR

Ashleigh VanHouten is a health and nutrition journalist, public speaker, certified health coach, and self-proclaimed health and fitness nerd. She has written for *Paleo Magazine* for more than eight years, along with a number of other health publications. She hosts the Muscle Maven Radio podcast, which has been downloaded more than 1.5 million times; for the show, she's interviewed some of the biggest names in health and wellness, including Dave Asprey, Steph Gaudreau, Laird Hamilton, and Mark Sisson. She's also worked with other top-rated health-related podcasts, such as Shrugged Collective, Muscle Intelligence, and Paleo Magazine Radio. Combining her formal education and professional experience in marketing and communications with her passion for healthy eating, exercise, and learning, Ashleigh works in a consulting role for a number of professionals in the health and wellness world, working alongside individuals like Dr. Gabrielle Lyon, Ben Pakulski, and Elle Russ.

As a kid, Ashleigh had two dream jobs: to be an author and to be an American Gladiator. Now that she's published her first cookbook, it's time to suit up and figure out her Gladiator nickname—suggestions welcome!